About ISTE

The International Society for Technology in Education (ISTE) is the premier non-profit organization serving educators and education leaders committed to empowering connected learners in a connected world. ISTE serves more than 100,000 education stakeholders throughout the world.

ISTE's innovative offerings include the ISTE Conference & Expo, one of the biggest, most comprehensive ed tech events in the world—as well as the widely adopted ISTE Standards for learning, teaching and leading in the digital age and a robust suite of professional learning resources, including webinars, online courses, consulting services for schools and districts, books, and peer-reviewed journals and publications. Visit iste.org to learn more.

Contents

MEETING COMMON CORE TECHNOLOGY STANDARDS

Strategies for Grades 9-12

Valerie Morrison | Stephanie Novak | Tim Vanderwerff

International Society for Technology in Education
EUGENE, OREGON • ARLINGTON, VA

Meeting Common Core Technology Standards
Powerful Strategies for Grades 9-12
Valerie Morrison, Stephanie Novak, and Tim Vanderwerff

© 2016 International Society for Technology in Education

Editor: Paul Wurster
Associate Editor: Emily Reed
Production Manager: Christine Longmuir
Copy Editors: Jennifer Weaver-Neist, Kristin Landon
Cover Design: Brianne Beigh
Book Design and Production: Jeff Puda

Library of Congress Cataloging-in-Publication Data

Names: Morrison, Valerie, author. | Novak, Stephanie (Stephanie M.), author. | Vanderwerff, Tim, author.

Title: Meeting common core technology standards : strategies for grades 9-12 / Valerie Morrison, Stephanie Novak, Tim Vanderwerff.

Description: First edition. | Eugene, Oregon : International Society for Technology in Education, [2016]

Identifiers: LCCN 2016001274 (print) | LCCN 2016006328 (ebook) | ISBN 9781564843715 (paperback) | ISBN 9781564845719 (Mobi) | ISBN 9781564845726 (ePub) | ISBN 9781564845733 (PDF)

Subjects: LCSH: Education, Secondary--United States--Computer-assisted instruction. | Educational technology--Study and teaching (Secondary)--United States. | Common Core State Standards (Education) | BISAC: EDUCATION / Teaching Methods & Materials / General. | EDUCATION / Computers & Technology.

Classification: LCC LB1028.5 .M6378 2016 (print) | LCC LB1028.5 (ebook) | DDC 371.33--dc23

LC record available at http://lccn.loc.gov/2016001274

First Edition

ISBN: 978-1-56484-371-5
Ebook version available

Printed in the United States of America

Chapter 7: **Implementing Practical Ideas**..58

Chapter 8: **Practical Ideas for Grades 9–10**...64

Chapter 9: **Practical Ideas for Grades 11–12**...94

References 130

About the Authors

VALERIE MORRISON graduated with an elementary education degree from Northern Illinois University (NIU) and began her career as a classroom teacher. She became interested in teaching with technology early on and was a computer teacher for two years at a K–8 private school. Morrison then switched to the public school system, where she obtained a master's degree in instructional technology with an emphasis in media literacy from NIU. She gained 14 years of experience as a technology director / technology integration specialist and technology coach. Morrison worked closely with teachers and students to plan and differentiate lessons and projects that integrate technology. She taught technology workshops and classes for teachers and oversaw the technology program at her school. (She loves working with kids, teachers, and technology!) Like her coauthor Tim Vanderwerff, Morrison regularly served on her district's technology committee, and was involved with integrating current state and district standards with the latest educational technologies. She presented at various conferences, including a presentation in Springfield, Illinois, to state legislators, where she and coauthor Stephanie Novak briefed legislators on how schools use technology. Morrison has recently switched career paths and is now teaching education classes at the college level; she enjoys using technology to teach the next generation of teachers. She also has time to write now, which allows her to further educate the current generation of teachers.

STEPHANIE NOVAK knew from a very young age that teaching and working with kids was the right career path for her. She graduated from Northern Illinois University with a master's degree in reading and earned a reading specialist certificate from National Louis University. Novak started teaching at the middle school level but eventually settled in the elementary school system. As a classroom teacher for 27 years and an extended-learning teacher and coach for the past seven years, she has always felt learning should be fun and meaningful. Novak was on her school district's technology committee for many years and regularly tried new technology in her classroom. As an instructional coach, she encouraged teachers to help students grow in their learning at a pace that allows for the most intellectual and personal growth. For the past two years, Novak guided Grade 1–5 teachers through the Common Core State Standards, teaching them how to blend these standards with rigorous curriculum and prepare students for the digital age. After many years in education, Novak recently retired. She now looks forward to applying her years of experience in a consulting capacity for administrators, teachers, and students. She also plans to continue to publish stories that describe her successful experiences in the field of education.

 **TIM VANDERWERFF** has an extensive background in teaching and technology that began in the '70s. Although writing this book was a new experience, trying out new experiences in education are second nature to him. After graduating from Illinois State University and then earning a master's in educational administration from Northern Illinois University, Vanderwerff saw many federal and state initiatives come and go in his 33 years of teaching. Starting as a classroom teacher in grades 2–5, he was on his school district's technology committee for many years and regularly tried new technology in his class during that time. Vanderwerff eventually moved to the library media center at his elementary school in 1987. He was the librarian and the technology teacher, and he provided tech support for the building for many years. In 2010, he was asked to be a teaching coach, which involved sitting in on grade-level team meetings, finding resources for the new Common Core State Standards, supporting individual teachers and teams in the classroom (both with technology and with the newest educational strategies), and advising new teachers. Vanderwerff is recently retired, allowing him to devote more time to writing about the field in which he is so passionate.

DEDICATIONS

For my mom and dad, who taught me the value of education.
  —Valerie Morrison

To Bill; all my family; my confidant, Kim; and my District 96 friends.
  —Stephanie Novak

To my family: Kim, Eric, Michael and Kristina.
  —Tim Vanderwerff

Acknowledgments

We are grateful for the contributions of our friends, teammates, colleagues, and assistants with whom we worked throughout the years and who helped us come up with ideas for our first four books–this series. Working with so many talented people, we appreciate the collaboration and teamwork that allowed us to learn a great deal about coaching and technology. We would especially like to thank Alice Schmitz for her invaluable contributions to the practical ideas chapters in this book (Grades 9–12).

We would also like to thank our families for all of their amazing support during the writing of this book series. During the many times we spent meeting, editing, and struggling to write, their unwavering support was truly appreciated.

Also, we would like to thank the editors and their staff at ISTE for their insight, guidance, and patience. Their ongoing support has been much appreciated as we've gotten familiar with the process of publishing.

Introduction

Have you ever found yourself sitting in a meeting wondering, "How am I ever going to change all my lessons to fit the new Common Core State Standards?" At that moment, you also realize your district wants you to integrate the latest digital-age technology, and that has you asking yourself, "Where will I get this technology? Will it be provided for me, or am I responsible for purchasing and providing the technology?"

All of this might seem overwhelming—what is a teacher to do? First, you might turn to your teammates and colleagues for help and support. Perhaps your district provides current technology development for staff on a regular basis and has instructional coaches to help teachers chart this new territory, planning new lessons, bringing in resources, and infusing technology. In reality, most districts don't have all of this support. Yet teachers are especially in need of technology when considering their clientele: students.

Until recently, every state was doing their own thing when it came to standards. The Common Core State Standards (CCSS) is a U.S. education initiative seeking to bring diverse state curricula into alignment with each other by following the principles of standards-based education reform. The CCSS is sponsored by the National Governors Association Center for Best Practices (NGA Center) and the Council of Chief

State School Officers (CCSSO), and a vast majority of the 50 U.S. states are members of the initiative. So, if you are in a Common Core state, there are big changes happening. Even if you're in a state that's not adopting Common Core, there is a high likelihood your curriculum will soon look very similar to the CCSS initiative.

We, as coaches, have an important role in helping you, the teachers, and your students during this transition. Our hope is that you are in a district that provides high-quality professional learning experiences regularly to help teachers understand the shift from existing state standards to the CCSS. Professional development, along with this book and its resources, will help you identify the changes you will need to make to guide your instruction using CCSS with technology and support you in transferring new knowledge and skills to the classroom. It is a large task, but focusing on specific goals for student learning utilizing the CCSS with technology will have a positive effect on student achievement. Moreover, it will improve your teaching.

CCSS were designed to prepare K–12 students for college and career success in the areas of English language arts, math, science, and social studies. CCSS defines the knowledge and skills students should have in their K–12 education, with an emphasis on learning goals as well as end-of-year expectations.

Most states have had English language arts and math standards in place for a few years. However, these standards vary, not only in coverage but also in levels of rigor. CCSS is very explicit about what is expected of students at each grade level. Students, parents, teachers, and school administrators can now work together toward common goals. CCSS will be consistent from school to school among states choosing to adopt the standards. If students or teachers transfer to different schools, they will all be assured that learning expectations will be the same. Any student, no matter where they live within a Common Core state, can be assured that they will be able to graduate from high school, get ready for college, and have a successful career.

The standards first launched in June 2009. State leaders from the CCSSO and NGA developed them together with parents, teachers, school administrators, and experts from across the country. Both national and international research and evidence informed development of the standards. After public comment, organizers released the final version of the CCSS in June 2010.

The CCSS were written in a clear, understandable, and consistent manner to align with college and work expectations. These standards contain rigorous content, as well as an application of knowledge through higher-order skills. CCSS are evidence based, and they build on the strengths and lessons of current state standards.

Writers of CCSS also gathered information and advice from top-performing countries to ensure that U.S. students are prepared to succeed in a global economy and society. Here is a helpful link from the Common Core State Standards Initiative's **"About the Standards"** page: **(http://tinyurl.com/26f7amp)**.

Transition to the Common Core will be a challenging task for your students as well as for you. With the implementation of these new standards, students will be expected to become self-directed and critical readers, writers, and thinkers. At the same time, you will need to make adjustments. In fact, you will need to shift your entire instructional practice.

Shifting your instructional practice will require a great deal of work and commitment, but this will all be well worth the effort for both you and your students. By breaking things down into small steps, the transition will seem less overwhelming.

This book is part of a collection of four books designed to help teachers connect technology to the Common Core in their classrooms. We learned how to do this by teaching together, and we have more than 85 years of combined teaching experience. As teammates, we worked with students, teachers, and administrators to integrate technology in the same school district. Our hope is that you will think of this book as your coach, because we can't be with you personally. We hope to show you how to integrate the newly embedded tech-related language found within the standards into your everyday curriculum.

In Chapter 1, we address some of the issues that your students face and discuss how important it is to tailor their learning experiences. Today's students are the first generation to truly grow up in the age of the internet, complete with emailing, texting, instant messaging, social networking, tweeting, and blogging. Teaching this new generation of children, teenagers, and young adults can be challenging because of how digital technology has affected their brains and behaviors. The Common Core curriculum has kept this new generation of students in mind, and so will we.

In Chapter 2, we explore the importance of engaging and educating parents. We follow this up with a discussion in Chapter 3 about the equipment you need to teach to the standards, and we show you how to address the roadblocks that stand between you and this technology. There are always roadblocks that educators commonly face, and we hope to show you how to get around them effectively so that you—and your students—can succeed. We should also mention that although we are sharing many tools and resources with you, we are not affiliated with any company. The programs, apps, and websites listed in this book are simply those that we feel support the standards.

In Chapter 4, we discuss effective staff development, and we explain in Chapter 5 how the CCSS is organized. Chapter 6 takes a deeper look at the specific standards for the grade level you teach. With these standards in mind, we show you how to begin and offer several classroom-tested lesson ideas in Chapters 7–9 that will ensure your students are satisfying the tech-related benchmarks outlined in the CCSS.

We realize that technology is constantly changing and that digital tools come and go. To make certain that you continue to have the most current resources at your fingertips, visit **our website (http://tinyurl.com/oexfhcv)**. The website password for the 9-12 book is: 9MCCTS12. There, you will find an updated list of the apps, software, and websites mentioned in this book.

Let's begin by taking a closer look at today's generation of tech-savvy students and the skills they bring to the classroom.

Chapter 1

Today's Students

A two-year-old taking a selfie? Seven-year-olds tweeting? No doubt about it, today's students come to school knowing more technology than ever before. New educational research suggests that offering a variety of learning opportunities, including lots of technology options, may be the best way to engage today's generation of learners. Educators need to respond to this generation and address their unique learning needs. We, the authors, believe this so passionately that we think a chapter about this subject is a must in any book about teaching children in the digital age. Technology must be made available to students. Technology must become ubiquitous.

The CCSS are designed to bring school systems into the new century. They are designed with the tech-savvy child in mind. Actually, the standards are designed with their future workplace in mind. That is the driving force behind the technology we see in the standards and why teaching to your students' future needs is extremely important. Please keep this mind as you read this chapter.

Who Are Your Students?

The students you now have in your classroom grew up using digital technology and mass media. According to Debra Szybinski, executive director at New York University's Faculty Resource Network, (http://tinyurl.com/pqwr7va), this generation is:

> ... a generation characterized by some as self-absorbed, attention-deficit-disordered, digital addicts who disrespect authority and assume that they can control what, when, and how they learn, and by others as smart, self-assured, technology wizards, who follow the rules, and who are on their way to becoming the powerhouse generation. Clearly, this is a generation like no other, and that has posed an entirely new set of challenges both in and out of the classroom for faculty members and administrators alike.

Some of you are part of this younger generation. If so, you were the first to truly grow up in the age of the internet: emailing, texting, instant messaging, and social networking. Yet the current generation is ever changing. Those born even 15 years ago did not have technology so pervasive that it was with them 24/7. Many students entering school now are completely immersed in technology outside of school.

Ironically, at many schools, there is a disconnect to students' real lives and their way of learning. Schools are often islands of 20th-century thinking in a 21st-century world. Schools must do a better job of reaching the current generation of students; they need to respond to and address students' unique learning needs. Technology needs to be constantly available to students at school.

What Does This Generation Know and Do?

Many children entering kindergarten now have access to desktop computers, smartphones, tablets, and/or laptops at home. These children begin using all or most of these devices by the time they are three years old. Whether you go to playgroups, parks, or wherever, you're likely to see young children who are working on their parents' tablets or smartphones (or begging to use them!). These students come to us with skills that include (but are not limited to) swiping to work an app; navigating a mouse to play computer games; operating their own electronic devices, such as children's learning tablets, handheld learning devices, and interactive video games; and hunting and pecking on the keyboard to send emails. Also, our tech savvy-students can take videos and photos using a tablet or smartphone, as well as converse with someone by texting, blogging, and messaging. Most have been exposed to the internet and understand that they can find almost any kind of information there.

Because they have so much information at the touch of a button and constant stimulation around them, this generation is often attempting to multitask. It makes sense to them to watch TV, send a text, and find out what the weather will be all at the same time!

Some say that the current generation has hovering parents and a sense of entitlement. While this may be taken as a negative, having parents who are involved with their children and their children's school is a good thing, as it strengthens the home-school connection. Students who have parents who are involved in their academic life can be better students, and they are less afraid to try new things. Educators need to recognize these traits and use them to help students reach their maximum potential.

Being social is very important to the students in this tech-savvy generation. They are certainly the "in touch" generation, with immediate access to texts, emails, social networking sites, and even the sound of a human voice at the other end of the line. This generation is lost when their smartphone or tablet breaks down; they feel "cut off from the world" when they don't have instant access to the internet.

How Has Technology Affected Students' Minds?

By the time they're in their 20s, today's students will have spent thousands of hours surfing the internet and playing video games. This vast amount of screen time seems to be shortening their attention spans. At a time when their brains are particularly sensitive to outside influences, excessive screen time affects the way they learn and absorb information.

Furthermore, this generation does not read books to find information. Online search engines are prevalent in providing all of the information they need quickly, without having to go through a book from cover to cover. With access to an overabundance of information, they need to be skilled hunters who know how to sift through data quickly and efficiently. This new learner doesn't necessarily read from left to right or from beginning to end. Visuals help today's students absorb more information than they do from straight text. Thus, students become better scanners, a useful skill when confronted with masses of online information in a world that's full of noise and multiple stimulations. So, most modern students have learned to block out distractions while they focus on the task at hand.

How Has Technology Affected Behavior?

Because of the constant use of technology, there is less and less face-to-face communication taking place. We all have seen instances of parents and children sitting next to each other without speaking at a restaurant. Instead, they simply sit and quietly engage with their individual tablets or smartphones.

There are many debates about how technology helps or harms the development of a student's thinking. Of course, this depends on what specific technology is used, as well as how and with what frequency it is used in school. Our duty as educators is to decide what technology to use in the classroom and when, because technology influences students' thought processes. Educators need be aware of this effect to guide students in becoming digital-age learners.

How Do We Move Beyond the ABCs?

Education has gone through a monumental transformation in the last 20 years. Some changes have greatly improved the way teachers educate, while others are still under evaluation. The great debate between play-based preschool versus learning-based preschool is a case in point. What we have found during our years as teachers is that to progress in the classroom, teachers have to adapt to the times, adopting new techniques while continuing to use time-tested methods. Success in teaching a new generation of students isn't based solely on what educators are teaching them but, rather, how educators are teaching them.

We have seen our share of success stories and our share of students who struggled for reasons that are completely preventable when these students have the right tools. For these highly activity-scheduled and gadget-oriented students, traditional one-size-fits-all teaching is no longer effective. Sitting behind a desk, listening to the teacher talk, and reading from a textbook are completely ineffective. This generation of students needs to be engaged in active and interactive learning to enhance their knowledge. They do not want technology just because it is "cool." They need technology because it drives their world now and will continue to drive their world in the future. They are looking for something dynamic to make learning come alive—to make it different and interesting every day. Being connected accomplishes that goal.

How Can Educators Succeed in the Digital Age?

Thinking that technology is a new toy that will go away or doesn't have a place in education is no longer an option. We educators need to embrace technology and tap into what our students are already coming to us with, using it to advance their learning. But this technology cannot just be digital worksheets!

This is not always easy, especially when students know more about how to use the technology than many teachers. Therefore, it is our duty to catch up and make sure we know what our students know. This can be done in many different ways; however, the easiest way is to do what they do: pick up tablets or smartphones and start playing with them! Once we have the background skills to know what our students know, we can move forward. We simply need to remember that technology is a tool. And we can use these tools like anything else we use in education—manipulatives in math, novels in reading, and microscopes in science, just to name a few.

Of course, this new reality being imposed on and by the current generation has implications for you as a teacher. It used to be that students conducted research by using books that were from credible publishers, and those books went through rigorous editing and fact checking. This generation uses the internet almost exclusively. If your students get all of their information from the internet, then you must teach them media literacy skills. This skill set has become extremely important in an information age where children need to discern fiction from fact on the internet when, sometimes, we adults have trouble differentiating it for ourselves.

You need to tap into what your students are experiencing every day and use it to your advantage. Many of your current students will work in very social settings but in a different way than previous generations. Let them work often as partners or in groups to create multimedia presentations or digital videos. Because they love to send emails and video chat, let them email, instant message, or video chat with students around the world! This generation is good at multitasking. Allow them to do more things at once, such as opening multiple screens while taking notes on a research paper. Students all know how to use a smartphone, so when on a field trip, let them record a video of what they are seeing. They are used to constant noise and stimulation. Do not make them work quietly at their desks; rather, they should work with hands-on activities like live apps or green-screen technology. Students know at a very young age how to navigate the internet. Let them run to the computer when they have a question instead of asking you for the answer.

We know this new generation of children, teenagers, and young adults can be challenging because of how digital technology has changed their way of learning and behaviors. The following chapters will further address some of these issues and how learning needs to be specialized, giving more examples of how to integrate technology with the new CCSS. The Common Core curriculum has kept this new generation of students in mind, and so will we.

Chapter 2

Parent Education

The past decade has been financially difficult for schools. States across the country have had to slash education budgets because of downturns in the economy. If your district's budget was not affected by financial cuts, it is among the few. As for the rest of us, we have had to achieve more with less. To make matters even more challenging, we now have new standards that ask schools to immerse students in technology—a very expensive task. Having parents on your side in this budget struggle can be very helpful.

In the years since the CCSS were written and adopted by most states, some attitudes toward the standards have changed. More recently, parents and community members have begun to question them. So it is important, as a teacher, to be proactive in getting the word out about what is going on in your classroom. Work with parents and the community to educate them about CCSS in your state, district, and school. Parents only want what is best for their children, and a little reassurance from you can go a long way.

This reassurance begins with listening to parents. Ask them about their concerns. Answering their questions with facts will help them to better understand why your state adopted the standards.

The following are just a few of the technology concerns that have been raised about the CCSS recently. Knowing about them and other controversial issues allows you to defuse concerns before they become major issues.

Why Do Parents Need to Know about Technology Standards?

You don't need technology to read and you don't need technology to do math—civilizations have been doing both for centuries. Nevertheless, you must admit that technology does help in both areas. If we were still at the turn of the last millennium (1000 AD), we would be hand-copying books. The printing press brought books to the commoner and education to those who wanted to learn. The abacus is fine but hardly as good as a calculator or a computer. Technology marches on so that we can advance, learn more, and pass that knowledge along to the next generation.

The computer revolution of the last century is finally hitting the classroom with the encouragement of the CCSS. Before these standards, the pervasive use of computers was for schools with money or those who could write winning grants. Even so, many schools that were thought to be advanced had not integrated technology into everyday learning. The Common Core is the first set of widely recognized standards to do that. But why do parents need to know about them? There are several reasons.

First, keeping students versed in the fundamentals of technology will enhance your teaching tremendously, and students' parents can help with this at home. Survey parents to see if they have internet access and broadband at home. What kind of equipment do they use—do they have cameras or video capabilities? What do they allow their children to use? Knowing what your students have or do not have at home evens the playing field in the classroom. Encourage parents to teach their children how to use tablets, computers, video cameras, and other mobile devices so students come more prepared to school.

Second, learning doesn't just happen at school. You need to educate parents because they are the main support system for learning away from school. Consistent, clear standards now put forward by CCSS enable more effective learning. Knowing what technology and what software will be used to master these standards greatly assists parents and, in turn, their children. Look at the **Harvard Family Involvement Network of Educators (FINE, http://tinyurl.com/hguh777)** for the latest research and insights on how to get students' parents involved.

Third, technology can instantly link parents to what their children are learning. Knowing assignments, communicating with teachers, and understanding what is expected are all improved with today's technology. There is even an article out there (DeWitt, 2013) about a principal who tried "flipping" parent communication, which you might try too. Whatever you implement is a win-win for you and your students. Take advantage of technology in communication; don't shun it. It will make your life easier.

Finally, we are becoming a smaller, more codependent world. To have a world-class education that keeps our nation and civilization moving forward, all students need to be well versed in the newest technology. That is what the CCSS are all about! The Common Core State Standards Initiative's mission statement affirms, "The standards are designed to be robust and relevant to the real world, reflecting the knowledge and skills that our young people need for success in college and careers" (Council of Chief State School Officers & National Governors Association Center for Best Practices, 2010). In other words, the CCSS is designed for your students' success as adults in the work world, where technology is integral.

Even so, parents must be a part of this endeavor or their children will still struggle to succeed. Involving them is as important to you as is any other aspect of your students' learning. Do not think of parent education in the CCSS as an add-on—a tool to be used if you have time. Investing in your students' parents and having them on your team benefits you and lessens your load. In a synthesis of studies done on families, communities, and schools, Henderson and Mapp (2002) stated, "Efforts to improve children's performance in school are much more effective if they encompass their families. Regardless of income level or education background, all families can—and often do—support their children's success." (p. 208)

What Issues Do Parents Have with Technology in CCSS?

Parents may ask you about some of the controversial things they are hearing in the news related to the Common Core. One controversy involves a misunderstanding about standards and curriculum. Standards describe what students should know; curriculum is how they get there. For example, even though there is no standard for cursive writing or keyboarding, that doesn't mean it won't be in your school's curriculum. Curriculum is still developed locally. Educate parents who are concerned that they have no control over their child's curriculum—they still have the ability to contribute to what is taught in their local school.

Another controversy centers on test scores from states that adopted the CCSS early on: scores decreased. Although it may or may not be true in your district, scores quite often decrease when the format of the tests changes. One example is when students go from paper-and-pencil tests to digital assessments. According to Swanson (2013), if your school changed tests, then a result might be decreased scores until students become familiar with the new format. The best way to combat this is to have other digital tests in the classroom throughout the year, to make your students feel more comfortable with the new format.

A common concern we have heard as teachers and as CCSS coaches is that the federal government will be able to collect the data of individual students because of these digital tests. This has been a particularly heightened apprehension recently. The fact is, there are laws passed by the U.S. Congress (2010) that prohibit the creation of a federal database with students' personally identifiable information. Although the law is in place, you should still be vigilant about keeping this sensitive data secure. You are the first line of defense and need to have procedures in place. Please go over your district's student privacy policy. If there is none, push hard to make one.

How Can Parents Help with Assessment Technology?

As the teacher, you should help parents and community members understand the types of questions and problems that students are asked to solve on the new digital assessments. During parent nights, open houses, and/or in newsletters, introduce parents to the **Partnership for Assessment of Readiness for College and Careers (PARCC, www.parcconline.org)** and **Smarter Balanced Assessment Consortium (www. smarterbalanced.org)** websites. You can download sample questions to show to parents; and it can also be helpful to put new assessment questions next to old assessment questions so everyone can directly observe the shift.

If your state is going to use the Smarter Balanced test, have parents use the sample questions at the PARCC site to test their children at home. The sample Smarter Balanced test can also be used to prepare for the PARCC test. Both tests' questions are similar and based on the CCSS.

Don't forget the basics. Make sure parents know what kind of equipment the students will be tested on, and have them use similar equipment at home if possible. This will make the device a secondary concern so your students can focus on the test. And send home a sample question weekly so parents can become familiar with the changing assessments. Make sure some of the sample test questions you send home require students to use technology to answer the question, as this will be included on the assessments.

How Can Parents Help Students Meet Technology Standards?

Parents need to see the value of having technologies at home that can help their children achieve more. At the same time, home technology will help you accomplish these new curriculum tasks that, as we teachers know, are daunting, to say the least.

A recent poll by the Leading Education by Advancing Digital (LEAD) Commission (2012, p. 23) found that parents and teachers believe students who lack home access to the internet are at a significant disadvantage. Home access to broadband is viewed as important to learning and doing well in school for the following reasons.

- Home access greatly exceeds anything that your students could ever bring home in their backpacks.

- Home access allows parents to become more involved in their child's schoolwork and allows for more effective communication between parents and schools, thus promoting greater student success.

- Having home access vastly expands the time your students can learn and explore.

- Home access leads to greater collaborative work engaging students in online group homework (This last point dovetails perfectly with many of the new CCSS technology initiatives).

Home access needs to have your active support. At the beginning of the year, run a workshop for parents about the kinds of technology you will be using and why. Teach parents how to monitor their children for internet safety as well. You may want to call on your library media specialist or tech specialist to help you if they are available in your school.

Of course, you may teach in an area where parents do not have the funds to have broadband access or technology at home. Following are a few ways to address the issue.

- For homes that have broadband but no computers/tablets, start a program that allows students to check out resources from the school overnight.

- Have after-school clubs or homework help where technology is available.

- Open the school in the evenings for parents and students, providing them access to teachers and to the technology they need.

- Apply for one of many grants available from different levels of government, foundations, and companies to help with your school community's access to technology.

Wherever you teach, parent education is the key to student success with the state standards. Lack of information is one of the main reasons parents are opposed to the CCSS. Being a proactive partner with them will defuse most objections that arise—from parents and from others in the community—and actually create proponents of what is going on in your classroom through this challenging time. Having parents as partners can only help when you are faced with technology needs, such as lack of hardware and software, lack of assistance, and gaps in your students' tech knowledge.

Parent education is only part of the puzzle, however; you must first educate yourself about the CCSS and technology before you can effectively educate anyone. To address this, we have included a chapter on staff development (Chapter 4). But before we explore your professional development options, let's take a closer look at the roadblocks you may encounter on your journey to get technology into your classroom.

Chapter 3

Roadblocks to Technology

U nless your school or district has unlimited funding and gives you completely free reign on your purchases, you have hit roadblocks in your quest for classroom technology. Chances are that you do not have the student technology to become a fully stocked digital-age learning environment, but you are not alone. In this chapter, we provide ideas to best use and manage the equipment and software/ apps you do have, and we explore ways to get more. It is our hope that when we come to the later chapters on practical ways to integrate your technology into the new Common Core curriculum, you will be better prepared to maximize your resources.

What Are the Roadblocks to Accessibility?

If it is not possible to provide all of your students with tablets or laptops, providing half the class access to this technology is the next best thing. This allows you to work with small groups or pairs of students. Another option is to share technology with the classroom next door to gain at least some time with a full class set of laptops or tablets.

Lack of funding for 10–12 Tablets/Laptops per Classroom

One option is to have each grade level share a cart of 15 laptops or tablets in addition to a roving cart that any classroom can access. We would suggest grade-level sharing of technology with no more than three sections, as more sections limit student use further. If there are four or more sections in a grade, more carts should be added. This will allow the grade level to have access to at least half a class set. When you need a full class set, use the mobile cart to fill in the gaps. Another way to share additional mobile devices is to divide the 15 laptops or tablets into sets of five for each of three classrooms and then have teachers share devices if a class needs more. You could also place all 15 laptops or tablets on a cart and provide a signup sheet for as-needed use.

Only 4–6 Laptops/Tablets per Classroom

You can have half the class double up on the tablets at one time or you can share with other classrooms near you to get more. To accomplish the latter, you have several options: you could pick a time every day when two or three classrooms share their laptops or tablets for an allotted amount of time; you could have certain days when you each have them; or you could ask for them informally. The key is easy accessibility.

Computer Lab Limitations

A computer lab with enough computers for all of your students is another great resource, especially if it includes a tech or media center teacher or assistant. This is great because everything is in a set location and there is another knowledgeable teacher available to help. The negative is that you have to sign up for certain times, and everyone must work on the computers at the same time. If you have access to tables in the lab or in a nearby learning space, however, you have the opportunity to do other things with students who have finished their work on the computer, forming smaller work groups as you would in a traditional classroom.

1:1 Initiatives

Many districts are moving to a 1:1 tablet model for tablets or laptops, but if this is not the case in your district, then you will be more limited. More than likely, you will not have a full class set to yourself. If you are able to get a set to share, the easiest arrangement is to schedule times to use the devices. However, with such limited class time and many students per class, splitting up a class set so teachers get four to five devices per class may be a better option. It will just take more planning on your part to outline how your students will divide up their technology time.

At this level, enlisting students' smartphones is another option. Many students have them and bring them to school. Your district should discuss how to use these resources to their advantage while not interfering with the learning process. Some states are already using student-owned devices in their schools and have begun writing policies for them. About.com has a great article about addressing cell phone issues in schools—**"Cell Phone Policy" by Derrick Meador, (http://tinyurl.com/ptb6eaz)**.

Additional Equipment

How do you choose additional technology to better equip your classroom when your budget is already tight or inadequate? Aside from laptops and tablets, it is imperative to have a multimedia projector so that all students can see lesson materials, projects, resources, and so on. Other equipment that is valuable includes:

- **Document cameras:** You will use these every day to display written books, worksheets, student work, and the like. Once you have one, you won't know how you got along without one!

- **Interactive whiteboards:** These are great for engaging students, especially during whole-group instruction.

We could have included interactive response systems as well; however, with so many new websites available that can turn your laptops, tablets, or smartphones into interactive technology, buying response systems is no longer necessary

Some interactive websites that are free (and may offer an upgrade for an affordable fee) are:

- Socrative: (www.socrative.com)
- Exit Ticket: (http://exitticket.org)
- Annotate: (https://annotate.net)

Keeping Up with Students' State Assessments

Different groups developed PARCC and Smarter Balanced to test for college and career readiness starting from Grade 3 onward. Your students may be tested three or four times a year. PARCC and Smarter Balanced (with very few exceptions) are the two main tests that states use to provide teachers the information they need to help students become successful with the Common Core standards. These two assessments are computerized and have certain technology requirements, but they allow traditional paper-and-pencil versions when necessary. (Teachers should still be aware that traditional versions may be phased out eventually.)

We will not address the specifics of network requirements; just know that your school or district will need to meet certain operating system and networking specifications whether they are using the Smarter Balanced or the PARCC assessment. Additionally, your network must be able to address security requirements to keep student information safe. Following are the informational sites to help you find what you will need.]

- **PARCC technical requirements: (http://tinyurl.com/jmhyrey)**
- **Smarter Balanced technical requirements: (http://tinyurl.com/nuaqy6u)**

How Do We Overcome Software and Hardware Roadblocks?

You cannot benefit from technology if you don't have it. It is also difficult to share it if you don't have enough of it. You need it on time and easily accessible if you truly want to use it seamlessly. This may be the biggest roadblock. We discussed above how you can use different configurations of new or existing hardware in your school. The more pervasive the technology, the easier it will be for you to achieve the goals set forth by the Common Core.

Sources of Funding

If you don't have enough equipment and/or software, you can apply for grants. While there are more grants available for economically disadvantaged districts, some are accessible to all districts. State and federal grants are available, for example, especially if you can link your needs to the Common Core. The Bill & Melinda Gates Foundation and big companies like Google, Target, and Staples give to schools. Many districts have foundations that grant teachers money. You could even do a fundraiser for your school for new technology. Following is a list that is by no means complete but offers a great place to start.

GOVERNMENT
- **21st Century Community Learning Centers (http://tinyurl.com/7nx37vb):** This funding is designed to get parents and the community to actively support your work in the classroom.

- **Individuals with Disabilities Education Act (IDEA, (http://tinyurl.com/77b2dwa):** These funds are for students with disabilities.

- **Grants.gov (http://tinyurl.com/k8fybkt):** Search this site for all available federal grants. These grants include:

  - Investing in Innovation Fund (i3)

  - Race to the Top Fund: The government provides grants for Race to the Top specifically for the CCSS.

  - Title I, Part A—Improving Basic Programs Operated by Local Educational Agencies

  - Title I, Section 1003(g)—School Improvement Grants (SIG)

  - Title I—Supplemental Education Services (SES)

  - Title I, Part C—Migrant Education

  - Title I, Part D—Prevention and Intervention Programs for Children and Youth Who Are Neglected, Delinquent, or At Risk

  - Title II—Professional Development

  - Title II, Part D—Enhancing Education Through Technology (EETT)

  - Title III—English Language Acquisition State Grants

  - Title VII, Part A—Indian Education

- **Computers for Learning (http://computersforlearning.gov):** This government program encourages agencies to transfer their used computers and related peripheral equipment directly to schools.

- **State Government (http://tinyurl.com/oexfhcv):** Look for your state's educational website in this online index.

FOUNDATIONS

- **Bill & Melinda Gates Foundation (http://tinyurl.com/odwcrra):** This is the largest, private foundation in the world. Its primary aim in the U.S. is to expand educational opportunities and access to information technology.

- **The Foundation Center (http://foundationcenter.org):** This independent, nonprofit, information clearinghouse collects information on foundations, corporate giving, and related subjects.

- **Foundations.org (http://tinyurl.com/7sf3c):** This online resource provides an A–Z directory of foundations and grant makers.

- **The NEA Foundation (http://tinyurl.com/or2qc56):** This teacher association gives grants in several areas.

COMPANIES

Many of the companies that manufacture the products we use every day have educational initiatives that offer grants for public schools. Following are just a few.

- **Target (http://tinyurl.com/cdt25kz):** Target offers grants in many areas, including: education, the arts, and public safety.

- **Toshiba (www.toshiba.com/taf/k5.jsp):** Toshiba also offers math and science grants for Grades K–5.

- **Google (http://tinyurl.com/pm9gar4):** Google has several sites dedicated to corporate giving. Google for Nonprofits is a good place to start your search.

- **Microsoft Corporate Citizenship (http://tinyurl.com/p62et7u):** These grants are available for after-school programs.

- **Staples Foundation (www.staplesfoundation.org):** Staples Foundation for Learning teaches, trains and inspires people from around the world by providing educational and job skill opportunities.

- **CenturyLink Clarke M. Williams Foundation's Teachers & Technology Program (http://tinyurl.com/otej8rl):** These grants are designed to help fund projects that advance student success through the innovative use of technology. Teachers in public or private PK–12 schools in CenturyLink's residential service areas are eligible to apply for a Teachers and Technology grant.

OTHER RESOURCES

- **National Charter School Resource Center (http://tinyurl.com/ph2ytng):** This resource website has many links to funding opportunities.

- **eSchool News (www.eschoolnews.com):** This is a great grant resource for K–12 and higher education.

- **Internet@Schools (http://tinyurl.com/nnh5n9d):** This online magazine for education provides a vast list of free resources, grants, and funding.

- **Scholastic (http://tinyurl.com/nd3t97t):** This educational mainstay has many great grant resources too.

Free Software and Apps

Software and app purchases are a challenging roadblock, especially if your district or school doesn't provide enough funding. Fortunately, there are many free resources. Search app stores and type in "free." Free sites, such as Google Docs, are also great places to start. In addition, there are entire sites with free services geared toward the CCSS.

If you are in a small district or a private school, or if you live in a state where funding is limited, follow the money. Go to websites in states and at schools that do have the funds. Look at websites in wealthier school districts near you. Do they have CCSS lessons, activities, and technology ideas that are free to anyone on the internet?

Many states have CCSS resources posted for free! Take advantage of them. For example, New York has many helpful suggestions at **engageNY.org (www.engageny. org/common-core-curriculum)**. Utah has also published a very resourceful Common Core site, which can be found at the **Utah Education Network (UEN, http://tinyurl. com/l2e532)**.

Free software and apps are also available from private companies. These sites usually have ads, or they may want you to purchase add-ons; you and your district will have to judge their value for yourselves. More examples of free applications and websites will be given in the "Practical Ideas" chapters of this book.

What Other Roadblocks Must We Solve?

Systemic educational roadblocks can take many forms, which are often unintended or unavoidable. Here are three common challenges teachers face.

Misguided Policies

Some districts or schools require that all departments have the same apps or software. They don't allow teachers to choose what they prefer, and this can be frustrating. If your district wants all software to be the same, you might try explaining why each department and each teacher would benefit from using different software, apps, and equipment appropriate to their students' needs.

Some districts implement policies that do not allow teachers to use technology as a tool. Instead, they force teachers to use technology when other mediums or tools make more sense. For example, we discovered a district that required teachers to teach with a tablet 85% of their instructional time. This district even required students to bring tablets to gym class and physical education teachers to use tablets in every class period. School leaders who enforce this kind of policy know very little about infusing technology into the classroom. It would be better to achieve higher technology use through staff development and individual coaching (for example, through the use of this book) than by generating untenable policies that don't actually affect meaningful student learning.

To counter these policies, speak to your principal, go to a technology meeting, or attend a board meeting! Explain that technology is a tool and that the CCSS does not expect you to use technology every second of the day. There is a time and place for technology just as there is a time and place for math manipulatives, a calculator, a book, and even a pencil. Balance is the key. If anything is overused, it (and your effort) is set up for failure.

Parents

Parents will ask the question, "Why do we need new technology?" Have a discussion at open house nights and board meetings about what you will be doing or would like to do with technology. Explain that the CCSS expects everyone to integrate technology, and this is important for today's students. Please refer to the chapter on parent education (Chapter 2), which has specific suggestions about many of the issues that become parental roadblocks.

Staff Development

Teacher training is so important. You need to have professional development in the area of technology for yourself as well as for your students. If you have a technology coach, great! Spend a lot of time with this coach—set up weekly meetings. They can help you as well as model or co-teach with you. There are many professional development opportunities online as well as off-site in the area of technology. Refer to Chapter 4 to learn how to get staff development outside your district and how best to get around these roadblocks!

How Do You Get the Help You Need?

One of the key components of using technology is getting help. It is easier for high school students to work independently with technology and follow directions. However, it may still be very difficult to manage a class of students who are all trying to use technology at the same time. This is also the case when teachers try to work with a small group while the rest of the class is doing something else on tablets. Inevitably, something goes wrong with someone's computer, so many high school districts use student technology assistants.

It is extremely helpful to have another set of hands. If you have assistants who come to you on a regular basis to help, this is a great resource. You can call on these assistants when you need them, which allows greater freedom to work with the whole class—if you have enough equipment.

If you do not have access to assistants, you might try using parent volunteers. The worst part of using volunteers is inconsistent attendance. However, if you can find a parent or two who is willing to come in on a regular basis, they can be a great help. You will need to find time to train your volunteers of course, but once you do, most will be savvy enough to pick up what they need to do in class.

Make sure that you post passwords where it is easy for students to find them. Forgotten passwords are an annoying occurrence, so having them easily accessible for all will help you manage the situation comfortably.

Another option is to work with your fellow teachers. Consider arranging your schedules so that you each take extra students while the other uses technology with a smaller group. Overseeing fewer students makes technology use much easier to manage.

Create peer groups that have a mix of tech-savvy students and those who struggle with technology. This is especially effective at the high school level. Making the most of available technology is all in the management of it.

Although there can be many roadblocks that prohibit you from using classroom technology the way that you would like, there are ways to overcome these challenges. By using the suggestions given in this chapter, we hope you will overcome any roadblocks that lie in your way and that you have most everything you need at your fingertips.

 **Chapter 4**

Staff Development

When technology integration is at its best, a child or a teacher doesn't stop to think that he or she is using a technology tool—it is second nature. And students are often more actively engaged in projects when technology tools are a seamless part of the learning process.

—"What Is Successful Technology Integration?" (Edutopia, 2007)

Without a doubt, today's student comes to school with a strong background and understanding of technology. This generation of tech-savvy students is interested, motivated, and even driven by technology. As you will see, CCSS has explicit technology standards within grade levels. But technology, as a tool, needs to be infused in all other CCSS standards as well. Having a tech savvy classroom for today's students is the best way to create a 21st-century learning environment.

Truly integrated technology is ever present but invisible. You can use technology as a tool for instruction—as a way to vary the way you present information. You also can provide technology options for students as a way for them to engage in content skills. And students in your class should be given opportunities to create and share their new learning with a myriad of technology tools. The CCSS are not just about presenting information to students; today's students need to be able to plan, reason, analyze, evaluate, and create. Technology integration in today's classroom will do just that—it will not only allow your students to become more engaged in the learning process but empower them to gain a deeper understanding of their learning.

A plethora of articles have been written about the success of CCSS and how good professional development for teachers and staff is a significant key to its success. Technology plays a very valuable role in guiding and fostering this effective professional development, as well as helping to boost current professional-development resources and practices. And technologies that make tools available to teachers on an ongoing basis present a solid jumping-off point for successful classroom integration.

Research has found that sending teachers to workshop-based professional development alone is not very effective. Approximately, 90–100% of teachers participate in workshop-style or in-service training sessions during a school year and through the summer. While workshops can be informational and timely, teachers need opportunities to implement new teaching techniques, not just learn about them. Thus, professional development needs to be ongoing and meaningful to your own professional circumstances. The most effective professional development also uses peer coaches and mentors to implement new learning in class.

How Do You Create a Technology Plan?

You need lots of support and tools to utilize and sustain technology in your classroom. If you do not have a district or school technology director or coach, how do you develop a plan to get yourself (as well as your fellow colleagues) what is needed? You can be the pioneer to get the technology ball rolling.

Following are suggestions to help you begin the journey of infusing technology in your classroom. Although this should not be your task alone, sometimes it falls to a single individual to blaze the trail. Fortunately, there are many online resources that can assist you with creating a technology plan. Edutopia is a well-known place to start, offering (among other things) **"Ten Steps to Effective Technology Staff Development" (http://tinyurl.com/oesjsmn).**

The first step is to put together a technology committee with as many representatives from different departments and grade levels as you can find. It would be great to include administration staff, as well as a district office representative. Parents, students, and outside technology experts can only enhance your committee.

Next, come up with some ways to show how you and your students can use technology in the classroom. Providing specific examples of students working with technology to address the ISTE Standards and the CCSS would be powerful!

Develop a detailed questionnaire for teachers to express their classroom needs, frustrations, and fears. This questionnaire can also serve as a place for teachers to describe what they hope to learn from professional development, including technology goals they would like students to pursue in class.

Ask students to describe the ideal state of technology in their classroom. Ask them how they envision the state of technology in their classroom in one year, two years, five years, and so on. Then place the ideas from this brainstorming session in a public document, so everyone on the committee and in the community can see and refer to it.

Lastly, conduct a teacher survey using the **ISTE Standards for Teachers** as a guide **(www.iste.org/standards/)**. These standards outline what teachers should know and be able to apply in order to teach effectively and grow professionally. ISTE has organized them into the following five categories:

1. Facilitate and inspire student learning and creativity

2. Design and develop digital-age learning experiences and assessments

3. Model digital-age work and learning

4. Promote and model digital citizenship and responsibility

5. Engage in professional growth and leadership

Each standard has four performance indicators that provide specific, measurable outcomes. You can use them to ascertain teachers' technology comfort level, attitude, and integration use in your school. Answers could be on a scale, such as "proficient enough to teach someone else," "able to hold my own," "a little knowledge," or "scared to death to even try." It may even be helpful to have teachers identify three to five areas that they feel are most important to improving technology within the year. Providing a space for them to write an explanation is also important, as they may not be able to rank themselves on a scale when they can't quantify what they don't know. Writing a paragraph about where they stand with technology might be easier for them. The data you gain from this survey should be shared with your building, other participating schools, the administration, and the district office. And you may want to consider repeating this comfort-level survey several times throughout the year.

Once you've determined the proficiency of staff members, you can enlist their help to create a digital folder of suggested lesson plans, activities, and projects for all to access and use. Your colleagues will not only be able to implement the folder's learning opportunities in their classrooms but add to the folder as they try new things. Something you may want to consider having is a reflection page to accompany any lesson, activity, or project posted. This will help others learn from and refine the ideas as they implement them on their own.

Additionally, your meetings, questionnaires, and survey results will identify teachers, staff members, parents, and administrators who have expertise in specific technology areas. Talk to your principal or district administrators to see if funding is available to pay for the planning time and workshops your experts may wish to lead. (As a rule of thumb, for every hour of professional-development class time, it takes at least two hours of planning.) Opportunities also need to be offered to your experts to advance their professional development. Perhaps you can even find a way to tap into the technology expertise of students, parents, and/or community members by having them lead some of your professional development workshops. Perhaps you can build in this professional development/collaboration time at least once a week. Carrying on conversations about the workshops at team meetings, staff meetings, even lunch is a great way to foster and gain interest in what you and your committee are doing.

Even if you are not willing or able to head up a technology committee, there are many things you can do to prepare your classroom for digital-age learning.

What Are Some Staff-Development Ideas?

Be creative in your pursuit of ongoing staff development. If you are pressed for time, observe other teachers who use technology in their classrooms. (Ask your principal, department head, or coach to find someone to cover your classroom so you can do this.) If you are fortunate enough to have a coach or staff-development person in your building or district, ask them to set up a weekly meeting with you to work on technology goals. If you do not have a coach, partner up with another teacher or two. Peer coaching, team teaching, peer modeling, or even just conferring with other teachers is a great way to advance your goals, objectives, and outcomes.

There are many conferences and workshops offered throughout the year. Check to see if your district will cover the expenses and provide substitutes so you and your colleagues can attend. Check out the **Bureau of Education & Research (BER) (www. ber.org)**; they are a sponsor of staff-development training for professional educators in the United States and Canada, offering many technology workshops and seminars about how to implement technology with the Common Core. There are also many technology grants offered by businesses. The magazines **Innovation & Tech Today (http://innotechtoday.com)** and **Tech & Learning (www.techlearning.com)** are good places to look for these opportunities.

Ask your principal to provide grade-level time for teachers to look at standards and plan how technology can be used. Then, as a group, develop activities, projects, and lessons that include technology; come up with management strategies for using technology; and (perhaps most important) decide how you are going to assess and evaluate students' learning. This team time is so important for you to brainstorm, share and develop ideas, and gather materials. Summer is also a good time for you and your colleagues to get together to collaborate and develop projects. Check with your district to see if they will provide paid time for your summer work.

Don't forget to share your own successes and those of others. Share disappointments as well so that others can learn from and refine them. Take pictures, write press releases, post on your school's website, and include what you are doing in your parent newsletters and emails. If possible, make a short presentation at a school board meeting. Who knows? You may gain the moral and financial support you're looking for! Share your successes any way you can!

Because needs continually change, keep planning and re-evaluating where you are and where you want to be. Encourage teachers to reach for the stars with their technology needs. Ask students how they feel about using technology and how it has affected their learning. These suggestions will help you and your colleagues get the technology you need.

Where Can You Learn about Staff Development?

There are a multitude of professional-development opportunities out there for technology, either in the workshop/conference format or online (accessible from the comfort of your home or classroom). Some opportunities are free, and some come with a membership fee to use the website or attend organization events. Others are priced per event. Following are a few suggestions.

ISTE (iste.org) has several fantastic staff-development resources, including its Professional Learning Networks (PLNs), which allow you to instantly connect with experts in your field from around the globe **(http://connect.iste.org/home)**. There are many different networks to join (depending on your professional interests) where you can ask questions, learn from colleagues, and get access to exclusive events and professional learning opportunities. ISTE also offers free Strategic Learning Programs with partners like NASA and Verizon, which can be brought to your school or district **(http://bit.ly/1PeJ97t)**. In addition, ISTE may have affiliate organizations in your area that provide professional development at seminars and conferences **(iste.org/affiliates)**.

EdTechTeacher (http://edtechteacher.org) is another organization that provides help to teachers and schools wishing to integrate technology to create student-centered, inquiry-based learning environments. They offer keynote presentations, hands-on workshops, online courses, and live webinars for teachers, schools, and school districts—all from your computer! What is nice about EdTechTeacher is that they understand teachers and students because the people leading the professional development have been or still are in the classroom.

Education World (www.educationworld.com) is a complete online resource that offers high-quality lesson plans, classroom materials, information on how to integrate technology in the classroom, as well as articles written by education experts— a great place for you to find and share ideas with other teachers.

Discovery Education (www.discoveryeducation.com) supplies a plethora of digital media that is immersive and engaging, bringing the world into the classroom to give every student a chance to experience fascinating people, places, and events. All of its content is aligned to standards that can be adjusted to support your specific curriculum and classroom instruction, regardless of what technology you have in your room. Discovery Education can help you transition to a digital-age environment and even replace all of your textbooks with digital resources, if that is your ultimate goal.

Because you are reading this book, you have already started your technology journey! And you are not alone in this nationwide endeavor. Kristi Meeuwse, an Apple Distinguished Educator, offers sage advice at her blog, **iTeach with iPads (http://iteachwithipads.net)**, as you begin your exciting learning adventure. You can also read about **"How Kristi Meeuwse Teaches with iPad"** at Apple.com **(http://tinyurl.com/qxzdsbu)**. Following is just a taste of her guidance:

> "Wherever you are in your classroom journey, it's important to reflect on where you are and where you've been. It's important to celebrate your successes, no matter how small, and then be willing to move forward and try new things. Daring to imagine the possibilities and being willing to change is not just transforming to your own teaching, it will transform your classroom in ways you never thought were possible. Today we will do exciting new things. Let's get to it."

—Kristi Meeuwse (2013, http://tinyurl.com/qf22zo7)

We will continue to give you more resources for staff development in the practical ideas chapters (8–9). To learn about staff development in grades other than 9–12, look for the three other titles in this series, as they provide information to help you differentiate for students at all levels of your class. Before we dive into lesson ideas for your specific grade and subjects, however, we will discuss how to effectively read, understand, and use the CCSS standards in the next three chapters.

 Chapter 5

Organization of the Standards

So your state or district has implemented CCSS, and you are asking, "Now what? How can I make this instructional shift, understand these targets, and provide quality instruction for my students?"

You can't make this transition if you don't know your way around the CCSS. So let's focus on the first task: understanding the organization of the standards. While reading this chapter, you might want to explore **"Read the Standards"** on the CCSS website **(http://tinyurl.com/p9zfnwo)** as we discuss the details.

How Are the ELA Standards Organized?

The English language arts (ELA) standards for Grades 6-12 are divided into seven parts (see Figure 5.1), five of which are comprehensive K-12 sections (grey boxes). Then there are two content area sections specific to Grades 6-12 (white boxes): one set for literacy skills in history/social studies and one set for science/technical subjects. The CCSS website's introduction to the ELA standards has its own **"How to Read the Standards"** section **(http://bit.ly/1ZgEHla)** that gives more information about organization as well as three appendices of supplemental material.

FIGURE 5.1. The CCSS English language arts standards

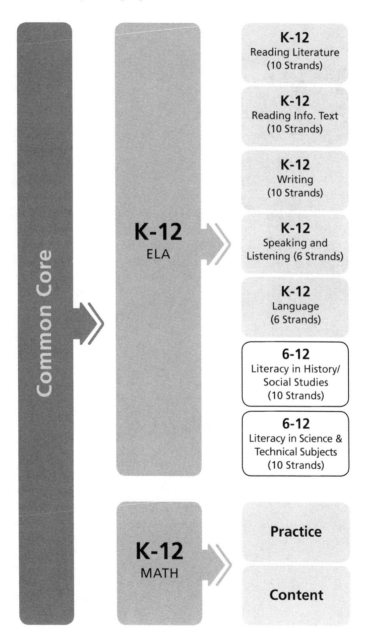

FIGURE 5.2. Figure 5.2. College and Career Readiness (CCR) anchor standard ELA 1 (CCSS.ELA-Literacy.CCRA.R.1) with grade-specific standards for Grades 9–12

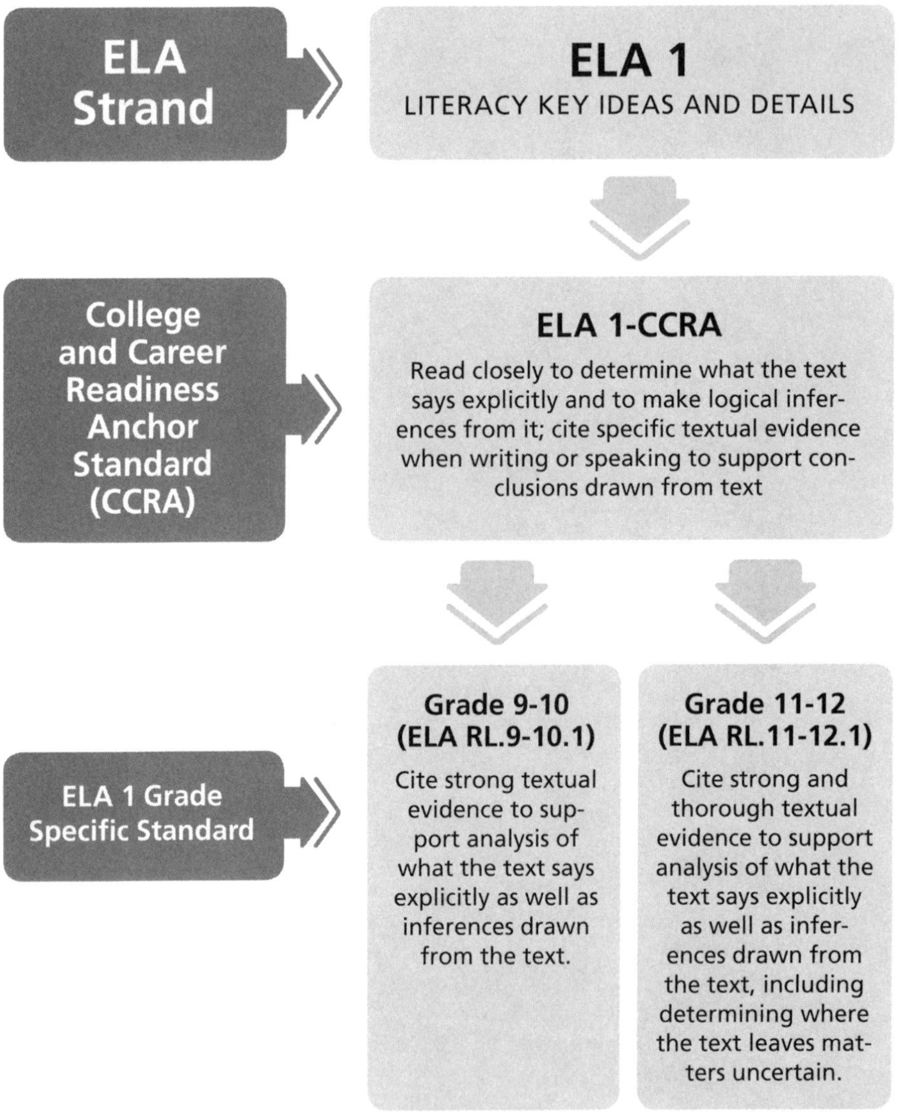

ELA Strand

ELA 1
LITERACY KEY IDEAS AND DETAILS

College and Career Readiness Anchor Standard (CCRA)

ELA 1-CCRA
Read closely to determine what the text says explicitly and to make logical inferences from it; cite specific textual evidence when writing or speaking to support conclusions drawn from text

ELA 1 Grade Specific Standard

Grade 9-10 (ELA RL.9-10.1)
Cite strong textual evidence to support analysis of what the text says explicitly as well as inferences drawn from the text.

Grade 11-12 (ELA RL.11-12.1)
Cite strong and thorough textual evidence to support analysis of what the text says explicitly as well as inferences drawn from the text, including determining where the text leaves matters uncertain.

Each section is divided into strands. At the beginning of each strand is a set of College and Career Readiness (CCR) anchor standards, which are the same across all grades and content areas. Take, for example, the first anchor standard illustrated in Figure 5.2: ELA 1 (CCSS.ELA-Literacy.CCRA.R.1). It is the same in Grade 9 as it is for a high school senior, but the grade-level standard is refined to what the student at each grade level is expected to accomplish within the anchor standard.

ELA 1 Anchor Standard: Read closely to determine what the text says explicitly and to make logical inferences from it; cite specific textual evidence when writing or speaking to support conclusions drawn from the text.

ELA 1 Standard in Grade 9 and 10: Cite strong and thorough textual evidence to support analysis of what the text says explicitly as well as inferences drawn from the text.

ELA 1 Standard in Grades 11 and 12: Cite strong and thorough textual evidence to support analysis of what the text says explicitly as well as inferences drawn from the text, including determining where the text leaves matters uncertain.

These anchor standards compliment the specific grade-level standards and define the skills and knowledge base that students should have by the end of each grade. The CCR standards are broad, while the grade-level standards provide specificity.

ELA standards focus on the following four areas:

1. Reading

2. Writing

3. Speaking and Listening

4. Language

The reading standards focus on text complexity (the difficulty of what students read), as well as the growth of their comprehension skills. Along with fictional stories and informational text, the CCSS focuses on poetry and dramas too. The writing standards delve into specific text types, reading response, and research. Some writing skills such as the ability to plan, revise, edit, and publish can be applied to most types of writing. Other writing skills are more specific: opinion and argumentation; informational explanatory texts, and narratives. Speaking and listening standards deal with collaboration and flexible communication. In this area, students acquire and refine their oral communication and interpersonal skills, perhaps through formal presentations.

The language standards concentrate on vocabulary, conventions, and effective use. This strand not only incorporates the essential "rules" of standard written and spoken English but also helps students to understand how language functions in different contexts. Making effective choices in meaning and style leads to better comprehension when reading and listening. The vocabulary part of this strand clarifies and/or determines the meaning of unknown and multiple-definition words and phrases by using the appropriate context clues and/or reference materials as needed. This strand also helps students demonstrate an understanding of figurative language, word relationships, and nuances in word meanings. In addition, students will be able to acquire and accurately use a range of general and domain-specific words and phrases in any academic area. (We'll talk more about domains later in this chapter, in the math standards section.)

With the organization in mind, let's learn how you, as an individual teacher, use the CCSS in the ELA.

How Do You Find ELA Standards by Subject and Grade?

Since most high school teachers teach just one or two subjects, the standards are organized so that you can focus on your specific area But it is very helpful to look back at the level before you and look ahead to the standards that come next to put your grade-level curriculum in context. (If you would like to look at a grade not included in this book, please refer to the other titles in this series.)

Using the main "English Language Arts Standards" page on the CCSS website is probably the most efficient way to find your grade- and subject-level standards (**www.corestandards.org/ELA-Literacy**). If you know what you are looking for, the corresponding reference numbers are useful. Here is a quick introduction:

All standards that relate to literature, informational text, writing, speaking, listening, language, history/social studies, and science begin with "CCSS.ELA-Literacy." The difference comes at the end, with the numbering system.

Let's use the following as an example.

CCSS.ELA-Literacy.RL.9-10.1

- **CCSS** is the abbreviation for Common Core State Standard.

- **ELA-Literacy** identifies this as an English language arts standard.

- **RL** stands for "reading literature."

- **9-10** is the grade range.

- **1** is the strand.

CCSS.ELA-Literacy.RH.11-12.5

- **CCSS.ELA-Literacy** represents the same information as in the previous example.

- **RH** means "reading history."

- **11-12** is the grade range.

- **5** is the strand.

But there are standards within standards that are not easily apparent at first glance. For instance, there may be a reading standard that uses historical or science text, or a speaking and listening standard that has a technology component to it. This book focuses on where technology is required in the CCSS, and there is plenty of technology to discuss in ELA and math!

You may be wondering how you will be able to keep all of this straight. After all, we haven't even started talking about math! We invite you to go online to view the math standards **(www.corestandards.org/Math)** as you read this next section.

How Does the Organization of Math Standards Differ?

When you look at the math standards, you will see immediately that they were written by a different group of individuals; they do not integrate other subjects like the ELA standards. Even the technology standard is separate. And the system of organization is different too. The authors of the math standards also state that the grade-level order can be changed. After the following overview, we will help you sort it all out.

For more than a decade, it has been widely reported that math curriculum in the United States is not even close to being on the same level as math education in high-performing countries. The consensus: U.S. math education needs to become substantially more focused and coherent to improve. To solve this, the CCSS were written to be clear, specific, and rigorous. Not only do the Common Core math standards stress conceptual understanding of key ideas but they continually return to the main organizing principles (place value and properties of operations) to structure those ideas. It is important to note that these new standards address what students should understand and be able to do in their study of mathematics. But asking a student to understand something also means asking a teacher to assess whether a student understands it. Therefore, we need to break apart these standards to enhance readability and to gauge what Common Core math comprehension looks like—so your students will be able to understand and you will be able to assess.

First, you need to understand that the standards provide a solid foundation before high school. They cover whole numbers, addition, subtraction, multiplication, division, fractions, and decimals, the study of ratios, proportions, and algebra. The standards require students in grades 9–12 to apply mathematical thinking to real-world problems. What this means to you and your students is that instead of covering a myriad of topics, your students will be required to immerse themselves in deep comprehension by applying mathematics to problems they have not encountered previously.

The CCSS for math begin with eight **Standards for Mathematical Practice (SMP, www.corestandards.org/Math/Practice)**, which apply to all grades, K–12. These standards represent ways in which students will be engaged with math content, processes, and proficiencies—longstanding, important practices. The eight SMP are:

1. Make sense of problems and persevere in solving them.

2. Reason abstractly and quantitatively.

3. Construct viable arguments and critique the reasoning of others.

4. Model with mathematics.

5. Use appropriate tools strategically.

6. Attend to precision.

7. Look for and make use of structure.

8. Look for and express regularity in repeated reasoning.

At the high school level, the standards outline the mathematics expected of all students to be "college and career ready" (like the CCR anchor standards in ELA, as discussed earlier). These high school standards also include additional mathematics for students who choose to take advanced-level courses. Standards at the high school level are organized by "conceptual categories" (versus grades), with each providing "a coherent view of high school mathematics." The six categories are:

- Number and Quantity

- Algebra

- Functions

- Modeling

- Geometry

- Statistics and Probability

Like the standards through eighth grade, the high school standards are still organized by domains. Domains are larger groups of related standards that are sometimes broken into clusters. Clusters are summarized groups of related standards that fall under the main standard (see the cluster that follows the standard in Figure 5.3). Due to the connected nature of math, you may see closely related clusters in other domains as well. (You can read more about this on the "How to Read Grade-Level Standards" page of the CCSS website's math standards introduction: **http://bit.ly/1sPykwd**.

Here is an example of how domains are used to organize the math standards:

CCSS.Math.Content.HSN.CN.C.7

- **CCSS** is the abbreviation for Common Core State Standard.

- **Math.Content** identifies that this is a math standard.

- **HSN.CN** is the domain (High School: Number and Quantity—The Complex Number System.

- **C.7** is the identifier for a related standard (or cluster) under the main standard—in this case "Use complex numbers in polynomial identities and equations" (see Figure 5.3).

Now that you know how to identify a high school math standard and its numbering system, let's look at the following figure to see the way in which this standard is actually presented in this domain.

TABLE 5.3. Example of a standard in the high school domain of Number and Quality—The Complex Number System

DOMAIN	STANDARD	CLUSTER
High School **Number and Quantity—The Complex Number System**	Use complex numbers in polynomial identities and equations.	CCSS.Math.Content.HSN.CN.C.7: Solve quadratic equations with real coefficients that have complex solutions. CCSS.Math.Content.HSN.CN.C.8: Extend polynomial identities to the complex numbers. CCSS.Math.Content.HSN.CN.C.9: Know the Fundamental Theorem of Algebra; show that it is true for quadratic polynomials.

The standard in Figure 5.3 defines what your students should know and be able to do after you taught and assessed that standard. Reading and familiarizing yourself with the standards will go a long way in helping you teach the standards later.

There are also SMPs that are part of the CCR anchor standards of the ELA. These standards are not overtly assessed but are necessary for you to include in your instruction. SMPs will not be the focus of this book except when they involve technology.

As you can see, math and ELA standards are written and organized very differently. We have tried our best to guide you through these differences, but we do recommend that you explore the resources we have provided here as well as others that we have referenced on **our website (http://tinyurl.com/oexfhcv)**. Here are two great resources that will explain the standards of mathematical practices: **http://tinyurl.com/l3zzsae, http://tinyurl.com/9ndshh6**. In the next chapter, we discuss technology and how it relates to the CCSS.

Chapter 6

Technology in the Common Core

This chapter focuses on the CCSS English language arts and math standards that have technology-related components written into them, first identifying and then analyzing these standards. This will prepare you for the later chapters, where we offer practical examples of how you can integrate these standards into your curriculum.

As CCSS coaches, we know that there are those of you who are excited about technology, those of you who think it is an annoyance, and those of you who fear it. These new standards will affect all of you because they force your districts and you, as teachers, to use technology more pervasively. Schools will feel pressure to address areas that may have been avoided in the past due to cost or apprehension. If you are a fan of technology, you will welcome the changes; if you are not, you will need to become proficient. You can no longer avoid technology in your classroom.

Where Is Technology in the ELA Standards?

The CCSS are designed to prepare students for college, the workforce, and a technology-rich society. And as you learned in the last chapter, the ELA standards have the CCR (College and Career Readiness) anchor standards—writing, reading,

ELA Standards (Grades 9–12) in Which Technology Appears

READING (9–12)

- CCR Reading (R) Standard 7 (**www.corestandards.org/ELA-Literacy/CCRA/R/7**).
  - Reading Literature (RL)
  - Reading Informational Text (RI)
  - Reading History (RH)
  - Reading Science and Technical Subjects (RST)

- CCR Reading Science and Technical Subjects (RST) Standard 9 (**http://tinyurl.com/jylor72**).

Note: While reading language (RL) and reading informational text (RI) are in all grades, reading history (RH) and reading science and technical subjects (RST) are in Grades 6-12 only. We will get into more detail about this and related anchor standard R.9 later in this chapter.

WRITING (9–12)

- CCR Writing (W) Standard 2 (**http://tinyurl.com/zt6kysv**).
  - Writing, History, Science, and Technical Subjects (WHST) Standard 2

- CCR Writing (W) Standard 6 (**http://tinyurl.com/zmxfdp8**).
  - Writing, History, Science, and Technical Subjects (WHST) Standard 6

- CCR Writing (W) Standard 8 (**http://tinyurl.com/jercjbv**).
  - Writing, History, Science, and Technical Subjects (WHST) Standard 8

Note: writing is an anchor standard throughout students' K-12 education, but an added strand of history, science, and technical subjects (WHST) is included from Grades 6-12.

SPEAKING AND LISTENING (9–12)

- CCR Speaking and Listening (SL) Standard 2 (**www.corestandards.org/ELA-Literacy/CCRA/SL/2**).

- CCR Speaking and Listening (SL) Standard 5 (**www.corestandards.org/ELA-Literacy/CCRA/SL/5**).

LANGUAGE (9–12)

- CCR Language (L) Standard 4 (**http://tinyurl.com/hmu54nx**).

Where Is Technology in the Math Standards?

As mentioned in Chapter 5, the math standards are written differently, and the technology standard in math (yes, just one standard) is separate from the rest of the math standards. However, this technology standard is meant to be used ubiquitously. Though many math standards do not overtly say that technology is required, if there is a need for a calculator or statistical analysis using a computer then that is what students should use. In math, the understanding is that these technology tools are used across grade levels and throughout the math standards even though there is only one written standard about it. (Note: This math standard is presented in detail after the grade-specific ELA standards at the end of this chapter.)

What about Using Technology in All Subjects?

Because technology is integrated throughout the CCSS, we should discuss in more depth what this actually means as you go about implementing the curriculum day to day. Though the standards give you specific language, the use of technology has been left wide open. They use terms like "digital tools," "other media," and "both print and digital" to let you, as the teacher, choose what is appropriate to the lesson. The new standards are trying to infuse technology into everyday classroom use, as opposed to having a separate period in a computer lab. Technology will need to become like the pencil: just another tool to choose from when students need to find the most appropriate one to complete the task at hand.

CCSS strongly encourages project-based lessons and is built to be cross-curricular. Also, Common Core is looking for higher-level thinking, learning, and application. All of these things lead to the use of technology as the most appropriate tool in many situations. They fit very well into the P21's (Partnership for 21st Century Learning's) **Framework for 21st Century Learning (http://tinyurl.com/nzvwyen)** and the **ISTE Standards for Students (www.iste.org/standards)**. If you have been working for some time on lessons that integrate technology and you think you will have to begin again, you will be relieved to know that the new standards are not so different.

How Do You Put ELA Technology Standards into Context?

When you look at the patterns of technology use in the standards, you improve your integration planning and learning achievement with these standards. Let's take a quick look at the technology patterns in the related Grade 9–12 standards.

R.7: This is the main technology standard in reading, but the CCSS does not expect students to use technology until grade 2. The standard then continues to develop in all subsequent grades, integrating and evaluating content in various technology formats that support the meaning of a story or literary work.

> **RL.7:** This standard begins in kindergarten, comparing illustrations and text, and then grows through the grades, using all types of media to compare, support, and analyze the story's meaning. Essentially, the purpose of the standard is to get meaning from more than the text. Meaning can also come from all the accompanying media and even the format of the story.

> **RI.7, RH.7**: These are similar to RL.7 but refer to informational text, history, and science and technical. Thus, you must keep in mind informational graphics—maps; photographs; diagrams; charts; and other media in history, **technology**, and science—and the way in which they augment information or help to solve a problem.

RST.9: This standard begins in Grades 6–8 with specific technology suggested, and it implies technology use in Grades 9–12. Students are asked to compare science and technical information they have studied with what they experience through experiments, simulations, videos, and other media, to build knowledge.

W.2: From drawing, writing, and telling about a topic in kindergarten, this standard evolves into producing a thesis in high school. It is your basic research paper that now includes an expectation to use any and all media that is appropriate to conveying the information.

W.6: This is one of the few anchor standards that is solely technology driven. From kindergarten through high school, students are required to use technology to collaborate with others when writing. Of course, this requires keyboarding skills, but they are not mentioned in the standard until Grade 3.

W.8: The use of technology in this standard is expected from Grade 3 through high school. It keys in on the gathering of information, the analysis of information, and the avoidance of plagiarism using multiple sources—digital as well as text—when writing informative or explanatory works. This standard works in tandem with standard W.2 and will probably be taught jointly.

WHST.2, WHST.6, WHST.8: These Grade 6–12 writing standards are similar to their W.2, W.6, and W.8 anchors, but the focus is on history, science, and technical subjects and the use of multimedia tools.

SL.2: This standard expects the use of technology from kindergarten through Grade 12. It is a listening standard, but in today's world, all kinds of diverse media are constantly available. Students need to be able to analyze and make decisions about this content.

SL.5: Beginning with the use of pictures when speaking in kindergarten, this standard builds to making strategic use of digital media for presentations in high school. Learning to use media in presentations is critical for college and career readiness.

L.4: This is a very straightforward standard that clarifies the meaning of words at all grade levels. Starting in second grade, students need to know how to find word meanings using not just print but digital dictionaries, glossaries, and thesauruses.

What about Assessment?

You don't begin a trip without an end in mind, and the end that must always be kept in mind with the CCSS is the standardized test your state will be administering. Whether it is the PARCC or Smarter Balanced assessment, or some other assessment your state is developing, there will certainly be a technology component to it. The tests will require some level of competence in selecting and highlighting text, dragging and dropping text, and moving objects on the screen. In the math areas of the test, tools that might be needed for the exam (calculators, rulers, a slide rule) will be available on the screen. Students may need headphones and a microphone to interact during the speaking-and-listening sections, and other multimedia may be used in other parts of the test.

The best way to prepare students is to know in advance the scope of technology they will need to master, but this will not be easy during the first years of rollout. Many things will be changing and many details will still be forthcoming. The tight deadline means your students may not be as fully prepared as you would like them to be. However, your preparation—giving students opportunities to use a myriad of technology as often as possible—will help them to be as ready as they can be for the assessments.

What Are the ELA standards with Technology?

The following is a listing of where technology appears in the CCSS. The first section contains the anchor standards, and the second section has the more specific grade-level standards. The standards are in order by level, so that you can find those that relate to the grade you teach more quickly. The part of the standard that pertains to technology is in boldface type. It is always helpful to look at the standards above and below your level to see where the students have come from and where they are going on their educational journey. Please refer to the other books in this series if you would like to see other grade levels.

READING
CCSS.ELA-Literacy.CCRA.R.7

R.7: Integrate and evaluate content presented in **diverse media and formats**, including visually and quantitatively, as well as in words.

Note R.9 as well: Analyze how two or more texts address similar themes or topics in order to build knowledge or to compare the approaches the authors take.

The R.9 anchor standard does not have any multimedia but does overtly include technology in its science and technical strand concerning the use of simulations, videos, and multimedia sources in Grades 6–8 (**RST.6-8.9**). Thus, when discussing sources for this standard in high school, digital sources (like those just mentioned) are implied.

WRITING
CCSS.ELA-Literacy.CCRA.W.6 and CCSS.ELA-Literacy.CCRA.W.8

W.6: Use technology, including the internet, to produce and publish writing and to interact and collaborate with others.

W.8: Gather relevant information from multiple print and **digital sources**, assess the credibility and accuracy of each source, and integrate the information while avoiding plagiarism.

Note: Anchor standard W.2 does not have multimedia but does include technology in that standard's strand starting in Grade 4 (**W.4.2.a**). This book focuses on **W.9-10.2.a**, **W.9-10.6**, **W.9-10.8**.

SPEAKING AND LISTENING
CCSS.ELA-Literacy.CCRA.SL.2 and CCSS.ELA-Literacy.CCRA.SL.5

SL.2: Integrate and evaluate information presented in **diverse media and formats**, including visually, quantitatively, and orally.

SL.5: Make strategic use of **digital media and visual displays** of data to express information and enhance understanding of presentations.

Even when your grade does not have a technology standard included in these main anchor strands (**R.7**, **W.2**, **W.6**, **W.8**, **SL.2**, **SL.5**, **L.4**), it is implied that it be used. We have listed here only those that state a technology use.

What Are the ELA Grade-Level Standards with Technology?

Following is where ELA grade-level standards appear in the CCSS (listed by grade). Note the following abbreviations: reading literature (RL), reading informational text (RI), writing (W), speaking and listening (SL), and language (L). We are including Grade 8 to give the technology standards some context. Please refer to the other books in this series to get a sense of the full scope of technology standards Grades K-12. (Note: as in the preceding section, the part of the standard that pertains to technology is in boldface type.)

GRADE 8

RL.8.7: Analyze the extent to which a filmed or live production of a story or drama stays faithful to or departs from the text or script, evaluating the choices made by the director or actors.

RI.8.7: Evaluate the advantages and disadvantages of using different mediums (e.g., print or **digital text, video, multimedia**) to present a particular topic or idea.

RH.6-8.7: Integrate visual information (e.g., in charts, graphs, photographs, videos, or maps) with other information in print and **digital texts**.

RST.6-8.9: Compare and contrast the information gained from experiments, **simulations, video, or multimedia** sources with that gained from reading a text on the same topic.

W.8.2.a: Introduce a topic clearly, previewing what is to follow; organize ideas, concepts, and information into broader categories; include formatting (e.g., headings), graphics (e.g., charts, tables), and **multimedia** when useful to aiding comprehension.

W.8.6: Use technology, including the internet, to produce and publish writing and present the relationships between information and ideas efficiently as well as to interact and collaborate with others.

W.8.8 and **WHST.6-8.8**: Gather relevant information from multiple print and **digital sources**, using search terms effectively; assess the credibility and accuracy of each source; and quote or paraphrase the data and conclusions of others while avoiding plagiarism and following a standard format for citation.

WHST.6-8.2.a: Introduce a topic clearly, previewing what is to follow; organize ideas, concepts, and information into broader categories as appropriate to achieving purpose; include formatting (e.g., headings), **graphics** (e.g., charts, tables), and **multimedia** when useful to aiding comprehension.

WHST.6-8.6: Use technology, including the internet, to produce and publish writing and present the relationships between information and ideas clearly and efficiently.

SL.8.2: Analyze the purpose of information presented in **diverse media and formats** (e.g., visually, quantitatively, orally) and evaluate the motives (e.g., social, commercial, political) behind its presentation.

SL.8.5: Integrate **multimedia and visual displays** into presentations to clarify information, strengthen claims and evidence, and add interest.

L.8.4.c: Consult general and specialized reference materials (e.g., dictionaries, glossaries, thesauruses), both print and **digital**, to find the pronunciation of a word or to determine or clarify its precise meaning or its part of speech.

GRADES 9–10

RL.9-10.7: Analyze the representation of a subject or a key scene in two different artistic mediums, including what is emphasized or absent in each treatment (e.g., Auden's Musée des Beaux Arts and Breughel's Landscape with the Fall of Icarus).

RI.9-10.7: Analyze various accounts of a subject told in different mediums (e.g., a person's life story in both print and **multimedia**), determining which details are emphasized in each account.

RH.9-10.7: Integrate quantitative or **technical analysis** (e.g., charts, research data) with qualitative analysis in print or **digital text**.

RST.9-10.7: Translate quantitative or **technical information** expressed in words in a text into **visual form** (e.g., a table or chart) and translate information expressed visually or mathematically (e.g., in an equation) into words.

RST.9-10.9: Compare and contrast findings presented in a text to those from other sources (including their own experiments), noting when the findings support or contradict previous explanations or accounts.

W.9-10.2.a. and **WHST.9-10.2.a:** Introduce a topic; organize complex ideas, concepts, and information to make important connections and distinctions; include formatting (e.g., headings), graphics (e.g., figures, tables), and **multimedia** when useful to aiding comprehension.

W.9-10.6 and **WHST.9-10.6:** **Use technology, including the internet**, to produce, publish, and update individual or shared writing products, taking advantage of technology's capacity to **link to other information** and to **display information flexibly and dynamically**.

W.9-10.8. and **WHST.9-10.8:** Gather relevant information from multiple authoritative print and **digital sources**, using advanced searches effectively; assess the usefulness of each source in answering the research question; integrate information into the text selectively to maintain the flow of ideas, avoiding plagiarism and following a standard format for citation.

SL.9-10.2: Integrate multiple sources of information presented in **diverse media or formats** (e.g., visually, quantitatively, orally) evaluating the credibility and accuracy of each source.

SL.9-10.5: Make strategic use of **digital media (e.g., textual, graphical, audio, visual, and interactive elements)** in presentations to enhance understanding of findings, reasoning, and evidence, and to add interest.

L.9-10.4.c: Consult general and specialized reference materials (e.g., dictionaries, glossaries, thesauruses), both print and **digital**, to find the pronunciation of a word or to determine or clarify its precise meaning, its part of speech, or its etymology.

GRADES 11–12

RL.11-12.7: Analyze multiple interpretations of a story, drama, or poem (e.g., recorded or live production of a play or recorded novel or poetry), evaluating how each version interprets the source text. (Include at least one play by Shakespeare and one play by an American dramatist.)

RI.11-12.7: Integrate and evaluate multiple sources of information presented in **different media or formats** (e.g., visually, quantitatively) as well as in words in order to address a question or solve a problem.

RH.11-12.7: Integrate and evaluate multiple sources of information presented in **diverse formats and media** (e.g., visually, quantitatively, as well as in words) in order to address a question or solve a problem.

RST.11-12.7: Integrate and evaluate multiple sources of information presented in **diverse formats and media** (e.g., quantitative data, **video, multimedia**) in order to address a question or solve a problem.

RST.11-12.9: Synthesize information from a range of sources (e.g., texts, experiments, **simulations**) into a coherent understanding of a process, phenomenon, or concept, resolving conflicting information when possible.

W.11-12.2.a and **WHST.11-12.2.a**: Introduce a topic; organize complex ideas, concepts, and information so that each new element builds on that which precedes it to create a unified whole; include formatting (e.g., headings), graphics (e.g., figures, tables), and **multimedia** when useful to aiding comprehension.

W.11-12.6 and **WHST.11-12.6**: **Use technology, including the internet**, to produce, publish, and update individual or shared writing products in response to ongoing feedback, including new arguments or information.

W.11-12.8 and **WHST.11-12.8**: Gather relevant information from multiple authoritative print and **digital sources** using advanced searches effectively; assess the strengths and limitations of each source in terms of the task, purpose, and audience; integrate information into the text selectively to maintain the flow of ideas, avoiding plagiarism and overreliance on any one source and following a standard format for citation.

SL.11-12.2: Integrate multiple sources of information presented in **diverse formats and media** (e.g., visually, quantitatively, orally) in order to make informed decisions and solve problems, evaluating the credibility and accuracy of each source and noting any discrepancies among the data.

SL.11-12.5: Make strategic use of **digital media** (e.g., textual, graphical, **audio, visual, and interactive elements**) in presentations to enhance understanding of findings, reasoning, and evidence and to add interest.

L.11-12.4.c: Consult general and specialized reference materials (e.g., dictionaries, glossaries, thesauruses), both print and **digital**, to find the pronunciation of a word or determine or clarify its precise meaning, its part of speech, its etymology, or its standard usage.

What Is the Math Standard with Technology?

The Standards for Mathematical Practice (SMP) are skills that all of your students should look to develop. As you learned in Chapter 5, there are eight SMP, which are designed to overlay the math content standards. In other words, the math practice standards apply to every one of the math content standards. So, although **MP5** is the only standard that includes technology, it actually means that every math content standard should use the appropriate tools, including tools that use technology.

Following is **MP5**, taken verbatim from the Common Core State Standards website. (*Note:* As in the preceding two sections, any text that pertains to technology is in boldface type.)

CCSS.Math.Practice.MP5

MP5: Use appropriate **tools** strategically.

Mathematically proficient students consider the available tools when solving a mathematical problem. These tools might include pencil and paper, concrete models, a ruler, a protractor, **a calculator, a spreadsheet, a computer algebra system, a statistical package, or dynamic geometry**

software. Proficient students are sufficiently familiar with tools appropriate for their grade or course to make sound decisions about when each of these tools might be helpful, recognizing both the insight to be gained and their limitations. For example, mathematically proficient high school students analyze graphs of functions and solutions generated using a **graphing calculator**. They detect possible errors by strategically using estimation and other mathematical knowledge. When making mathematical models, they know that technology can enable them to visualize the results of varying assumptions, explore consequences, and compare predictions with data. Mathematically proficient students at various grade levels are able to identify relevant external mathematical resources, such as **digital content located on a website**, and use them to pose or solve problems. They are able to use technological tools to explore and deepen their understanding of concepts.

It is important to note the standard's emphasis on using technology pervasively. Keep technology in mind, not only when teaching the standards but in the assessment, as it creates a learning advantage for your students.

We hope you have taken away important information on where technology can be found in the CCSS. In the next chapter, we discuss practical strategies and offer helpful resources so you can begin teaching the CCSS right away.

Chapter 7

Implementing Practical Ideas

Our world and education are changing rapidly. Without question, one size does not fit all in teaching. We know you work hard to personalize the learning in your classroom to reflect the individual needs, capabilities, and learning styles of your students so they have opportunities to reach their maximum potential. With this in mind, why not create tech-savvy classrooms for today's students?

In this chapter, we address practical ways to use new technology ideas within your classroom. Most of your students already come to school with a strong background and understanding of technology. They are interested, motivated, and even driven by technology. Having a tech-savvy classroom for today's students is the best way to create a digital-age learning environment.

How and Where Do I Begin?

Whether you are a new teacher, a teacher in the middle of a career, or a veteran teacher with just a few years before retirement, you will begin at the same place in respect to technology. To bring technology into your classrooms and your students into the digital age, you must give up your role at the front of class and let technology be a primary source of information. This journey calls for no longer teaching in the way you've been teaching and instead becoming facilitators of your classroom and the information presented there. Embrace all of the devices you have ignored or struggled to keep out of your classroom. Introduce yourself to new concepts that may not have existed when you were in school.

First, sign up for as many technology teaching blogs and websites as you can find. One website definitely worth a look is **Power My Learning (PowerMyLearning.org)**. There are many free activities for you to explore, and you can search for lessons by the CCSS. This website also allows you to build classes, assign and monitor student work, and customize playlists for your classroom.

Blogs are becoming an increasingly pervasive and persistent influence in people's lives. They are a great way to allow individual participation in the marketplace of ideas around the world. Teachers have picked up on the creative use of this technology and put the blog to work in the classroom. The education blog can be a powerful and effective tool for students and teachers. **Edutopia** has a wonderful technology blog **(http://tinyurl.com/p33sd7b)**. **Scholastic** also offers a blog for teachers, PK–12, **(http://tinyurl.com/oaaycar)**, and on a wide variety of educational topics.

Edmodo (www.edmodo.com) is a free and easy blog for students and teachers to communicate back and forth. We have given you links to all of these resources on **our website (http://tinyurl.com/oexfhcv)**. Teachers can post assignments, and students can respond to the teacher, as well as to each other, either in the classroom or at home. Students have the ability to also post questions to the teacher or one another, if they need help.

What Strategies Can I Use?

Get a routine going. Engage students in independent and self-directed learning activities. This is a great way to begin integrating technology in your classroom. All activities can be tied to your curriculum targets, and a couple of them can be technology based. There are a plethora of computer based games that you can bring to a center rotation. **IXL (www.ixl.com/math/)** and **MathPickle (www.mathpickle.com)** are two programs that support Common Core and can be used on computers or tablets.

If you are a high school math instructor, differentiated math meets the needs of all learners. It consists of whole-group mini lessons, guided math groups, independent learning stations with a wide variety of activities, and ongoing assessment. Independent learning is a great way to infuse technology into lessons. For more information on how to set up a guided math classroom check out the book *Guided Math: A Framework for Mathematics Instruction* (2009) by Laney Sammons, or view her **guided math slide presentation** online **(http://www.slideshare.net/ggierhart/ guided-math-powerpointbytheauthorofguidedmath)**.

For high school ELA instructors, having students work in small groups or independent practice that involves reading, writing, or vocabulary are opportunities to use technologies. All activities can be tied to your curriculum targets and can be technology based. Instead of having students writing in a journal, have them blog. Instead of students reacting or reviewing another student's work (using paper and pencil), have them use interactive response systems or Google forms. Programs and aps such as Google Docs, Prezi, Edmodo, and Explain Everything are just a few resources you can use to meet standards and bring writing into your ELA curriculum. Your students are using technology to be creative!

Flipping the classroom is another great way to integrate technology into your classroom. This teaching model, which uses both online and face-to-face instruction, is transforming education. Flipping is an educational strategy that provides students with the chance to access information within a subject outside of the classroom. Instead of students listening in class to content and then practicing that concept outside of the school day, that traditional practice is flipped. Students work with information whenever it best fits their schedule, and as many times as necessary for learning to occur. Inside the flipped classroom, teachers and students engage in discussion, practice, or experiential learning. By creating online tutorials of your instruction, using some of the tools mentioned in this book, you can spend valuable class time assisting students with homework, conferencing about learning, or simply being available for student questions.

Pick an app or program you are interested in bringing into your classroom. Play and explore. See what the possibilities are for using this technology in your classroom. You and your students can be technology pioneers. Allow your students to problem solve and seek new knowledge on their own, and then have them share with you. A great resource to use is **iPad in Education (www.apple.com/education/ipad)**, where you can learn more about how to teach with and use iPads in your classroom. This site from Apple gives you lots of information about what the iPad is capable of, gives examples of iPad lessons done by other teachers, and offers free apps!

How Do I Determine What Works Best?

Perhaps the next place to look is the **ISTE Standards for Students**, which were developed by the International Society for Technology in Education (ISTE) and can be found on their website **(www.iste.org/standards)**. These standards are a great framework to help you plan lessons and projects to support the Common Core technology standards in literacy, math, and critical thinking skills.

The Partnership for 21st Century Skills developed a Framework for 21st Century Learning. This framework identifies key skills known as the 4Cs: Critical Thinking, Collaboration, Communication, and Creativity. Table 7.1 takes those four skills and overlays them with digital resources that you can use in ELA. For instance, if you are a ninth grade teacher and want to use Collaboration in your lesson, you might try any of the seven digital resources suggested to plan your lesson: Google Docs, Popplet, GarageBand, Wixie, Edmodo, wikis, and Google Sites. These are suggestions, but there are many more apps and sites that might also fit well. You might notice that the 4Cs mirror many of the ISTE standards. This table is included to get you to think about how you can include the 4Cs and technology in your daily lesson planning.

Being an expert on all of the apps or programs listed in Table 7.1 is not necessary. Start with one you know, or find out which ones your students are familiar with and start there. Think about the target or lesson you want to teach. What is the goal? What technology device or app or program will support your teaching? Create an end product to show your students what you expect. Instead of step-by-step

TABLE 7.1. How Digital Resources for ELA Fit into the 4C's.

GRADE	CRITICAL THINKING	COLLABORATION	COMMUNICATION	CREATIVITY
9-12	Feedly Connected Learning Newsmap Learning Network	Edmodo Popplet GarageBand Wikis Google Sites	Show Me Skype Edmodo Explain Every-thing GarageBand	Microsoft Office GarageBand iMovie Keynote

teaching of the technology, it is important to let the students explore and discover for themselves, as long as your end product and expectations have been met.

You can also teach yourself about many of the apps or programs available by searching for them online. YouTube has step-by-step how-to videos for many tech apps and programs. Have your students show what they know by creating samples for you. Save everything you, your colleagues, or your students create, and keep it all in a digital portfolio, so you can share the samples with your students for years to come.

With an active learning environment and providing the tools your students need for 21st-century learning, watch the difference you will make as learning in your classroom skyrockets. All of this new technology is transforming today's classrooms. Social networking and mobile learning are just a few tech-related activities that students and teachers are embracing. The **website for this book (http://tinyurl. com/oexfhcv)** contains further lists of resources for how to incorporate the technology you have (or want to have) and ways for your students to learn and interact with them. In the following chapters, we further explore the standards for 9–12 that incorporate technology, suggest specific applications and strategies, and provide lessons to help students successfully achieve those standards.

Chapter 8

Practical Ideas for Grades 9–10

We realize that you will want to focus on your particular grade or subject when you are planning your lessons and implementing CCSS, so we have organized the Practical Ideas chapters by grade level, then subject. Each grade starts with an overview followed by ELA technology standards with accompanying apps, software, and websites that you can use to help your students have success with that standard. We then continue with the math standard for the grade level and offer appropriate resources. Finally, we have included some sample lessons for each grade level in various subject areas. Although we intend for you to seek your specific grade and subject to help you implement CCSS for your students, please do not disregard other sections of this chapter. To see grades other than 9–12, look for our three additional titles in this series, as they could provide information to help you differentiate for your students.

The CCSS has been set up to encourage cross-curricular work in English language arts. It standardizes the writing process through all classes in freshman through senior year by bringing the same writing standard into history, science, and technical subjects. The CCSS in high school is divided in two: 9–10 and 11–12. As a high school teacher, you understand the difficulty of working with colleagues in other departments. There are systemic roadblocks that make communication with other departments difficult in most high schools.

It is important to understand that history, science, and technical teachers communicating and co-designing lessons with language arts teachers will not only create a great foundation for your students as they prepare for college, it will also help you as a teacher working with the Common Core. Working together with colleagues in other departments may seem to be more work—and it may initially be more difficult—but it will actually ease your burden in the end. It is also important to work with your administrators to ensure that you have time to plan. Planning can take place during a school or districtwide professional development day or during staff meetings. Of course, the best option is to build collaboration time into the regular schedule.

Math is also an area where the technological tools become more varied and complex as students advance. The math standards are meant to be embedded in and a natural part of the units your students will be studying. Choosing the correct math tools will become an important part of your class's learning. There are wonderful new math resources available to help students become proficient with the standards.

Resources for Reading Literature

> **RL.9-10.7** | READING LITERATURE
>
> Analyze the representation of a subject or a key scene in two different artistic mediums, including what is emphasized or absent in each treatment (e.g., Auden's "Musée des Beaux Arts" and Breughel's "Landscape with the Fall of Icarus").

> **RI.9-10.7** | READING LITERATURE
>
> Analyze various accounts of a subject told in different mediums (e.g., a person's life story in both print and **multimedia**), determining which details are emphasized in each account.

THIS STANDARD BEGINS IN KINDERGARTEN with comparing illustrations and text and grows through the grades using all types of media to compare, support, and analyze their story's meaning. So, the standard is essentially to get meaning from more than the text. Meaning can also come from all the accompanying media and even the format of the story writing or media. It would be a perfect time to team up with the art teachers to create a cross-curricular unit of study.

This standard can lead to many creative projects. Students could focus on a poem, drama, play, artwork, or narrative, and it could be in a digital medium (movie, audio file, photograph, etc.). In fact, a digital medium would be one of the easiest forms to use when contrasting two forms of the same subject, since there are so many resources out there to use.

Of course programs such as **Microsoft Office (www.office.com), Apple Pages (www. apple.com/mac/pages)**, or **Google Docs (www.google.com/docs/about)**, to name a few, can be used to create the text and organize the media. Google Docs has a real-time collaboration component that is not found in the other programs and is very useful for group projects.

Your school district may subscribe to **Gale Literature Resource Center** or other Gale products **(http://tinyurl.com/o47ydvs)**. These are fine sources for thousands of frequently studied works. Your public library may have many digital resources that are free to your school district. Following are some excellent media resources.

MEDIA SITES

- **YouTube (www.youtube.com):** There are many free videos that your students can view, including literature, reviews of art, and endless other topics that might fit your curriculum. There is also a free app.

- **iTunes U (http://tinyurl.com/lbjbarh):** As stated on the Apple website, "Choose from more than 750,000 free lectures, videos, books, and other resources on thousands of subjects from Algebra to Zoology." It is accessed through iTunes free. A free iTunes U app is available.

- **SchoolTube (www.schooltube.com):** This is educators' best free source for a video-sharing community where students can watch or post videos.

- **Netflix (www.netflix.com):** Find filmed movies of classic literature, more current literature, and Shakespeare at this site. $8.99/month.

- **NeoK12 (www.neok12.com)**: This is a website with short stories on video.

- **PBS Learning Media (pbslearningmedia.org):** This site is a great source for classroom-ready, free digital resources at all grades and in all subjects.

- **National Gallery of Art (www.nga.gov):** This is the website for our national art museum in Washington. There are many resources, including more than 45,000 digitalized images from the national collection. All access is free.

- **New York Art Resources Consortium (www.nyarc.org):** Containing artwork from three major New York art museums, this free website has many pieces of art and art resources.

- **Louvre Museum (www.louvre.fr):** This famous French art museum has many great works available free online. They are accompanied by explanations of the works, and some give close-up details. A great resource.

Resources for Reading Informational Text

RI.9-10.7	READING INFORMATION

Analyze various accounts of a subject told in different mediums (e.g., a person's life story in both print and **multimedia**), determining which details are emphasized in each account.

OF COURSE, BIOGRAPHIES ARE A natural for this area. Although it is not required through the CCSS, this can be a great jumping-off point if you are a history, science, or technical teacher (such as art, music, home economics, or government) to take a subject your students are learning about and analyzing it through text. Documentaries, digital images of primary documents, opinion blogs, and more will allow students to gain differing perspectives and a more complete idea of the issues they are studying. Your class should also look at charts, maps, graphs, and data presented in any text and be able to gain meaning (by text we mean any textbook, PDF, website, pamphlet, brochure, etc.). If you are a writing teacher, and can't coordinate with other departments, you might think of using what your students are now learning in their other subject areas, to read and analyze informational text in your classroom.

Following are some software options we recommend for high school reading.

WEBSITES FOR INFORMATIONAL TEXT

- **Have Fun with History (www.havefunwithhistory.com):** This website is free and offers many short videos about historical events that can be used in the classroom. Some ads.

- **Library of Congress (http://tinyurl.com/2knoku):** This site, as part of the Library of Congress's website, has easily searchable access to thousands of digital resources from the history of the United States. Free.

- **Internet Archive (www.archive.org):** This site has more than 12 million books, films, audio files, photos, songs, and documents that are free to all. They come from libraries worldwide, TV stations, radio stations, and many other for-profit and nonprofit groups.

- **Bio (www.biography.com):** There are some good resources on this site for biographies, including text, photos, and video of various subjects. Some of the subject matter may be graphic. The site does have ads.

- **Time (www.time.com):** Time magazine's website has short biographies of Time's top 100 most influential people organized by year. Many of them have video clips of the subject. A great resource for current biographies. Free.

- **Feedly (www.feedly.com):** Organize any information on the web through this free app and website. It is a great resource for STEM to follow current events, scientific breakthroughs, etc. Find and follow any source of information.

Resources for Reading Historical and Technical Texts

RH.9-10.7	READING HISTORY, SCIENCE, AND TECHNICAL SUBJECTS

Integrate quantitative or technical analysis (e.g., charts, research data) with qualitative analysis in print or **digital text**.

RST.9-10.7	READING HISTORY, SCIENCE, AND TECHNICAL SUBJECTS

Translate quantitative or technical information expressed in words in a text into **visual form** (e.g., a table or chart) and translate information expressed **visually** or mathematically (e.g., in an equation) into words.

RST.9-10.9	READING HISTORY, SCIENCE, AND TECHNICAL SUBJECTS

Compare and contrast findings presented in a text to those from **other sources** (including their own experiments), noting when the findings support or contradict previous explanations or accounts.

RH.9-10.7 AND RST.9-10.7 ARE SIMILAR in that they focus more on quantitative and technical information your students would deal with in reading historical and technical texts. Thus, you must keep in mind informational graphics such as maps, photographs, diagrams, charts, and other media in history, science, and technical subjects and how they augment the information being given or help to explain or solve a social or scientific problem or event.

RST.9-10.9 also involves comprehension of technical information; the difference is in the comparison and contrasting of what is read to other sources. So your students are being asked to look at test results, surveys, and studies to come to a conclusion about what they have read on the subject.

Translating words into visuals and visuals into words has become easier with technology. In this standard, you are also asked to include charts, tables, and multimedia when aiding comprehension. Using programs like **Microsoft Excel (www.office.com), Apple Numbers (www.apple.com/mac/numbers)**, or **Google Sheets (www.google.com/sheets/about)** is a great way to create charts, graphs, and tables. Making their own charts and graphs helps students learn how to interpret and present information.

Following are some other useful apps, programs, and websites to help students become proficient in this standard. Using these resources, students will become more adept at manipulating, comparing, and interpreting statistical results.

APPS AND WEBSITES FOR READING TECHNICAL LITERACY

- **ChartGizmo (www.chartgizmo.com):** With your free account from ChartGizmo, you can start creating dynamic charts from static or collected data and place them on your website in minutes.

- **Gliffy (www.gliffy.com), Create-a-Graph (http://tinyurl.com/yoedjn),** and **Class-Tools (www.classtools.net)** are free sites you can use. Charts have never been so easy or so much fun!

- **Feedly (www.feedly.com/i/welcome):** Organize any information on the web through this free app and website. It is a great resource for STEM to follow current events, scientific breakthroughs, and so on. Find and follow any source of information.

- **Gooru (www.gooru.org):** This is a free website with a supportive app also available free. The idea of the site is to share information and to make great resources available globally. The Gooru site covers math, science, social studies, and language arts by providing videos, worksheets, assessments, and other resources for students broken out by each standard. Great for flipping the classroom.

- **Notability (www.gingerlabs.com):** This note-taking app allows your students to draw, using handwriting, typing, and importing text and other media. It allows markup of PDFs, too. It includes a word processor for essays, outlines, and forms. This app is $4.99.

- **iAnnotate (iAnnotate.com):** Similar to Notability, this app is primarily for note taking and markup of PDFs, PPT, and docs. It is a bit easier to import other formats than on Notability. The price is $9.99.

- **Evernote (www.evernote.com):** This free app allows you to import a worksheet, document, or picture, including a snapshot of a webpage, and then annotate it using tools that you would use with interactive whiteboard software. It lets you highlight words, cut and paste, and add sticky notes. It also allows you to use voice recognition. You can then send your annotated sheet to someone else.

- **Explain Everything (www.explaineverything.com):** This $2.99 app uses text, video, pictures, and voice to present whatever your students are asked to create. They can use graphs and illustrate an experiment with a chart or include historical documents and maps with their presentations to recount and explain the information.

Writing Resources

W.9-10.2.A	WRITING *and*
WHST.9-10.2.A	WRITING HISTORY, SCIENCE, AND TECHNICAL SUBJECTS

Introduce a topic; organize complex ideas, concepts, and information to make important connections and distinctions; include formatting (e.g., headings), **graphics** (e.g., figures, tables), and **multimedia** when useful to aiding comprehension.

W.9-10.6	WRITING *and*
WHST.9-10.6	WRITING HISTORY, SCIENCE, AND TECHNICAL SUBJECTS

Use **technology**, including the Internet, to produce, publish, and update individual or shared writing products, taking advantage of **technology's** capacity to link to other information and to display information flexibly and dynamically.

W.9-10.8	WRITING *and*
WHST.9-10.8	WRITING HISTORY, SCIENCE, AND TECHNICAL SUBJECTS

Gather relevant information from multiple authoritative print and **digital sources**, using advanced searches effectively; assess the usefulness of each source in answering the research question; integrate information into the text selectively to maintain the flow of ideas, avoiding plagiarism and following a standard format for citation.

FOLLOWING ARE SOME WELL-DESIGNED products that will help your students become more effective in the writing standards for these grades. Writing Standard 2 is the "how to write a paper" standard. Your students have been experiencing informative or explanatory writing since kindergarten. But, as they reach this level, they need to become college and career ready. They have to step up their game. Using an outlining program is a wonderful way for students to organize their ideas, concepts, and information. Several fine software programs have been used for mind-mapping and outlining for many years. However, there are also free sites available. There are even templates, such as a Venn diagram that allows students to compare and contrast and show cause and effect.

Writing Standard 6 is one of the few anchor standards that is solely technology driven. Students from kindergarten to high school seniors are required to use technology to collaborate with others when writing. In eighth grade, students produce and publish, but ninth grade will be the first time they will be required to "update" their writing and to "display information flexibly and dynamically." Updating their writing requires students to revise, react, and, in the case of argument, to rethink their position when more information is found about the topic. Flexible and dynamic display of information is easily accomplished if students are already using well-constructed programs, apps, and websites.

Writing Standard 8 starts in Grade 3 and continues through high school. This writing standard keys in on gathering information, analyzing it, and avoiding plagiarism using multiple sources, digital as well as text, when writing informative or explanatory works. The standard does change slightly between the eighth grade standard and its 9–10 matching standard. First, they add the term "advanced" when searching effectively online. Next, instead of the "proper use of quoting and paraphrasing" as in eighth grade, the standard changes to integration of information "into the text selectively to maintain the flow of ideas." Students will need to demonstrate that they know advanced search techniques. You will also need to have your students become proficient at maintaining the flow of their writing while using others' written or spoken words or ideas.

Following are some well-designed products that will help your students become more effective in the writing standards for these grades.

WEBSITES AND PROGRAMS FOR OUTLINING

- **iThoughts (www.toketaware.com):** Students can use this $9.99 mind-mapping app to organize their writing and presentation ideas. It has good import and export capabilities (PDF, PowerPoint, and other formats). This app can also be used as a whiteboard.

- **Inspiration Maps (www.inspiration.com/inspmaps):** This $9.99 app helps students organize, plan, and build thinking skills as well as create and analyze charts and other data by producing a mind map that can include text, video, photos, audio, and so on. Volume discounts are available. Their web-based version is called **Webspiration (http://tinyurl.com/bmop3nh)**. $6/month.

- **Bubble.us (www.bubble.us):** This is a free (with limited use) mind-mapping website for Grades K–12. It can be shared by multiple students at a time and comes with an app. For more options, purchase a package for $6/month or $59/year. Both come with a 30-day free trial. Site licensing is available. Contact the company for specifics.

- **Mindmeister (www.mindmeister.com/education):** This is a free, basic, mind-mapping website for Grades 2–12. Upgrades are available ($18/month for a single user; $30 per user for 6 months). Educational pricing is available for schools and universities ($6 per user for 6 months). All of the upgrades have a free trial period.

- **FreeMind (http://tinyurl.com/5qrd5):** This is a free mind-mapping tool for Grades 2–12. However, FreeMind is written in Java and will run on almost any system with a Java runtime environment. Options for a basic or maximum install are available.

WEBSITES FOR WRITING

We recommend the following websites for writing and note taking.

- **Google Drive (www.google.com/drive):** This website offers many useful tools free, including the following.

  - **Google Docs:** This is a great product to use for your students. It makes collaboration easy, especially from home. Students are also able to add pictures and short video clips, tables, and charts. These can be used to enhance the development of the main ideas or theme of their writing or presentations.

  - **Google Slides:** This is a simpler version of Microsoft's PowerPoint. Students can use this for sharing projects, summarizing their work, and peer-to-peer teaching.

  - **Google Sites:** Use this tool to create websites to display your students' research or to create WebQuests.

  - **Google Spreadsheet:** This tool can be used in many subject areas, to share data, charts, graphs, and other data for analysis of topics or issues.

  - **Google Blogger:** This blogging site has more features than Edmodo. Students can see other classes and can be cross-grouped with similar sections of the same course by ability or with mixed ability as needed.

  - **Google Form:** Great for checking student understanding instantly, getting any kind of feedback on issues being studied, and for peer-to-peer teaching.

- **Google Drawing:** This provides your students a place to create art, illustrations, graphics, diagrams, and so on, to enhance presentations and meaning in their language, history, science, technical, and mathematical work.

- **Add-ons:** Google has created many add-ons that can be attached to Doc, Spreadsheets, Blogger, Forms, and so forth to add targeted functionality. One example is Doctopus. This add-on allows teachers to instantly distribute documents to their class, which then show up in each student's folder. They can then use those documents as a starting point in assignments, discussions, or practice.

- **Edmodo (www.edmodo.com):** A free website where teachers can create a safe, password-protected learning community, including blogs and sharing documents. This is a great way to get students to write daily. A free app is available.

- **Wikispaces (www.wikispaces.com):** A free website where teachers can create a safe, password-protected learning community including blogs and shared documents.

- **EasyBib (www.easybib.com):** Students can use this free website and app to generate citations in MLA, APA, and Chicago formats easily. Just copy and paste or scan the book's barcode.

- **Citation Machine (www.citationmachine.net):** A free website students can use to generate citations in MLA, APA, Turabian, and Chicago formats easily. Just copy, paste, and the website does the rest.

- **Purdue Online Writing Lab (http://tinyurl.com/n8r94uf):** This website was developed for college students but is available to all free. It has resources for any kind of writing, grammar, spelling, and mechanics.

- **Gooru (www.gooru.org):** This is a free website with a supportive app that is also available free. The idea of the site is to share information and to make great resources available globally. They cover math, science, social studies, and language arts by providing videos, worksheets, assessments, and other resources for students broken out by each standard. Great for flipping the classroom.

- **CAST UDL Book Builder (http://bookbuilder.cast.org):** Use this nonprofit website to create, share, publish, and read digital books that engage and support diverse learners according to their individual needs, interests, and skills. The site is free.

- **Lulu (www.lulu.com) and Lulu Jr (www.lulujr.com):** These sites allow you to create real books and publish them online. Parents and students can purchase the bowoks. The site is free to use, but a fee is required to publish..

- **Wix (www.wix.com):** This online website creator is drag-and-drop easy and includes templates. The basics are free. An app is available.

- **Webs (www.webs.com):** This online website creator allows you to choose a template and then drag and drop elements onto webpages. Basic functionality is free, and an app is available.

- **Kafafa (www.kafafa.com):** This is another online website creator that is drag-and-drop easy and includes templates. The website is $9.99/month for a class.

- **Weebly (www.weebly.com):** This online website creator is also drag-and-drop easy and includes templates. The basics, which include five pages, are free. There is even an app available.

APPS FOR WRITING

There are many apps designed to improve student writing and note taking. The following are a few of our favorites.

- **Turnitin (www.turnitin.com):** This free app allows teachers to grade student writing anywhere and also gives an "originality report" on the student's work automatically. Teachers can grade with an interactive rubric, embed comments and audio, and highlight sections of the writing.

- **Peer Edit (http://tinyurl.com/hxzp5xk):** Let your students edit each other's work and learn writing in the process. This $3.99 app provides an organized support system for students to be able to practice peer editing with writing samples.

- **Notability (www.gingerlabs.com):** This note-taking app allows your students to draw, using handwriting, typing, and importing text and other media. It allows markup of PDFs, too. It includes a word processor for essays, outlines, and forms. This app is $4.99.

- **iAnnotate (www.iAnnotate.com):** Similar to Notability, this app is primarily for note taking and markup of PDFs, PPT, and docs. The price is $9.99.

- **Book Creator (redjumper.net/bookcreator/):** This versatile app can be used to have your students create their own ebooks with pictures, audio, drawing, text, video, and music. Easy for young children to use, but sophisticated enough for high school. Price is $4.99.

- **iBooks Author (www.apple.com/ibooks-author):** Apple has created a free app and/or program that is easy enough for young children, but complex enough for adults to create their own books. There are templates, ways to add interactivity, photo galleries, and more. This app gives you all you need to create your own professional-looking digital book.

- **Explain Everything (www.explaineverything.com):** This $2.99 app uses text, video, pictures, and voice to present whatever your students are asked to create. Students can animate, draw, or import most any file and share multiple ways.

Speaking and Listening Resources

SL.9-10.2	SPEAKING AND LISTENING

Integrate multiple sources of information presented in **diverse media or formats** (e.g., visually, quantitatively, orally) evaluating the credibility and accuracy of each source.

SL.9-10.5	SPEAKING AND LISTENING

Make strategic use of **digital media (e.g., textual, graphical, audio, visual, and interactive elements)** in presentations to enhance understanding of findings, reasoning, and evidence and to add interest.

SPEAKING AND LISTENING STANDARD 2 expects the use of technology from kindergarten through Grade 12. In today's world, we listen to all kinds of diverse media and constantly need to analyze and make decisions about its content. We also use multiple kinds of technology to speak to others. The idea behind Writing Standard 2 changes slightly between middle school and ninth and tenth grades from one of "analyzing" sources and evaluation of the "motives" behind sources to "integrating" sources and evaluation of "credibility" of sources. These are nuances that can be achieved through rubrics and even a simple use of student reactions to the credibility of the text they just read.

Speaking and Listening Standard 5 begins with using pictures when speaking in kindergarten. This standard builds to making strategic use of digital media for presentations in high school. Learning to use media to help in presentations is critical for college and career readiness. Your ninth and tenth grade students need to make strategic use of digital media to enhance understanding for them and their audience. This highlights using technology effectively, not just using it because it is something "awesome."

APPS FOR PRESENTATIONS

Traditionally Microsoft PowerPoint has been the presentation program of choice. There is now a free single version called Microsoft Online that includes Power-Point. Although this is still a great program to use, other, similar presentation programs have emerged. Apple offers **Keynote (www.apple.com/mac/keynote)** as part of its computer software package, but the iPad/iPod version does cost. Its features are very similar to PowerPoint. Another program that has emerged is the free **Google Slides (www.google.com/slides/about/)**. There are other resources that help with presentations, such as **Microsoft Draw (www.office.com)** and **Google Drawings (www.google.com/drive)**. Office is aimed toward business presentations; however, Google Drive products like Slides and Drawings are free and web based. Slides is also very easy to share and multiple users can work on it at once, even from home, which makes this an especially good program to use when interacting and collaborating with others. You are also able to add audio recordings to your slides as well as visual displays, such as pictures and short video clips. You could also have your students use the following digital tools.

- **Explain Everything (www.explaineverything.com):** This $2.99 app uses text, video, pictures, and voice to present whatever your students are asked to create. Whether it is writing or presenting, this app can do almost everything well.

- **Teach by Knowmia (http://tinyurl.com/omd28eu):** This free app will help you create lessons with text, pictures, videos, drawing, and audio that can be shared with students, and students can create their own peer-to-peer lessons. All can be uploaded and shared via Knowmia's website.

- **iMovie and iMovie Trailer (www.apple.com/ios/imovie):** This powerful program ($14.99) also comes as an app for $4.99. Students can use it to create presentations, movies, documentaries, and motion slideshows. Students can also create short (90-second) trailers that focus on important points about issues and events studied.

- **TouchCast (www.touchcast.com):** This cool and free app video creator lets you embed linkable websites, pictures, video, photos, and more into your video. It is also available on PC. There is some concern about privacy. TouchCast does have the EduCast channel, which is geared to education with teacher tutorials and other resources.

- **Aurasma (www.aurasma.com):** You can use this free app to take a picture, website, and so on, and add layers of animation to the original image. The company provides many resources, or you can use ones you create. Aurasma is great for getting information across in a quick, vivid, and animated way.

- **Glogster (www.glogster.com):** Presentations that you can create and share are available with this free app. You can browse and use those made by others. They provide images, graphics, videos, or upload your own. The companion website has teacher pricing of $39 to $99/year.

- **Prezi (www.prezi.com):** Create more engaging and effective presentations with a difference. Zoom in to any detail, or zoom out to show the big picture. Can present in a nonlinear way. Access your Prezi from anywhere. Import and export is easy in this free app.

- **BaiBoard (www.baiboard.com):** This whiteboard app allows students to create, collaborate, and share, and it's free. The difference between this and other whiteboard apps is that multiple students can have real-time access to one project and collaborate together.

Following are some software options we recommend you explore for high school presentations.

WEBSITES FOR PRESENTATIONS

- **Google Slides (www.google.com/slides/about):** This is a simpler version of Microsoft's PowerPoint, and it's free. Students can use this for sharing projects, summarizing their work, and peer-to-peer teaching.

- **Google Blogger (www.blogger.com):** This free blog site has numerous features. Students can see other classes and can be cross-grouped with similar sections of the same course by ability or with mixed ability as needed. There is an app available.

- **Google Hangouts (www.plus.google.com/hangouts):** This program can connect people and places around the world in a video conference. It allows multiple "callers" at one time. Free.

- **Edmodo (www.edmodo.com):** A free website where teachers can create a safe, password-protected learning community including blogs and sharing documents. App available for free.

- **Wikispaces (Wikispaces.com):** A free website where teachers can create a safe, password-protected learning community including blogs and shared documents.

- **Feedly (www.feedly.com):** Organize any information on the web through this free app and website. It is a great resource for STEM to follow current events, scientific breakthroughs, and so on. Find and follow any source of information.

- **Mural (www.mural.ly):** This website can help organize ideas more quickly and display and share information with others. You can use visual aids for presentations, and it works with other apps and sites. The website does cost, but there is special yearly pricing for students ($49), teachers ($199), and schools ($999).

- **Animoto (www.animoto.com):** This website allows you to turn your photos and music into stunning video slideshows. Educational use is free for unlimited videos of 20 minutes.

- **Tiki-Toki (www.tiki-toki.com):** Make engaging timelines with this free website (there are ads). You can embed videos, share with others, add photos, use color coding, and add 3D effects. Upgrade (no ads and 50 student accounts) for $125/year.

- **Zeega (zeega.com):** Easily combine media from the cloud to tell a story with video, audio, pictures, animation, and so on, to create a visual narrative. This mashup website is free, and students will enjoy the ease of this media-driven format to help get their story/poem/report message to others.

- **Capzles (www.capzles.com):** This is a free website, which has free apps to make it mobile. Students or teachers can create a digital presentation with video, photos, music, blogs, and documents.

- **WebQuest (www.webquest.org):** WebQuests are great tools to use for presentations. WebQuest is a website that allows students to follow an already-created, project-based lesson where information is found solely on the internet. You can also create your own WebQuest if you have a website building program or a website like Kafafa (www.kafafa.com/kafafa). WebQuest.org is the original and most popular site; however, if you search the internet, you will find more sites that you can use.

Language Resources

> **L.9-10.4c** | LANGUAGE
>
> Consult general and specialized reference materials (e.g., dictionaries, glossaries, thesauruses), both print and **digital**, to find the pronunciation of a word or determine or clarify its precise meaning, its part of speech, or its etymology.

THIS STANDARD IS VERY STRAIGHTFORWARD. It clarifies the meaning of words at all grade levels. Students need to know how to find word meanings using not just print but digital dictionaries, glossaries, and thesauruses. In ninth and tenth grades, the standard changes slightly, adding "its part of speech, or its etymology." The technology aspect of the standard is still the same.

DIGITAL DICTIONARY AND THESAURUS WEBSITES

- **Merriam-Webster (www.merriam-webster.com):** A free digital dictionary for all ages. It is the most commonly used digital dictionary and includes a thesaurus.

- **WordSmyth (www.wordsmyth.net):** This site shows three levels of a student dictionary. When looking up a word, there are also links to a thesaurus and rhyming dictionary for that word. You can sign up for an ad-free version, which will not cost your school.

- **Word Central (www.wordcentral.com):** A student online dictionary that includes an audio pronunciation of the word as well as the definition. There are many teacher resources.

- **Thesaurus.com (www.thesaurus.com):** This is a great thesaurus site with many extra features. It does have some ads. Available online and as an app. Free.

- **Online Etymology Dictionary (www.etymonline.com):** This free site gives a detailed etymology for most words. There are several ways to search from a single term to a phrase.

These sites should be bookmarked or put on your website for easy access. The more students use them, the more comfortable they will become. You should do lessons and activities to learn and practice how to find parts of speech and etymology with an online dictionary.

Math Resources

MP5	MATH

Use appropriate **tools** strategically.

THERE ARE TWO MAIN SETS OF STANDARDS, processes and practices, for the Common Core Math standards. First, you have the math targets, written similarly to ELA (Number and Quantity, Algebra, Functions, Modeling, Geometry, and Statistics and Probability). While you work with high school students on mathematical processes, such as Algebra or Modeling, you need to teach your students how to apply the Standards for Mathematical Practices (which include problem solving and precision) to those processes. One practice, the only one that includes technology, is mathematical practice 5, "Use appropriate tools strategically."

Following is the explanation CCSS provides for **MP5**.

> Mathematically proficient students consider the available tools when solving a mathematical problem. These tools might include pencil and paper, concrete models, a ruler, a protractor, **a calculator, a spreadsheet, a computer algebra system, a statistical package, or dynamic geometry software**. Proficient students are sufficiently familiar with tools appropriate for their grade or course to make sound decisions about when each of these tools might be helpful, recognizing both the insight to be gained and their limitations. For example, mathematically proficient high school students analyze graphs of functions and solutions generated using a **graphing calculator**. They detect possible errors by strategically using estimation and other mathematical knowledge. When making mathematical models, they know that **technology** can enable them to visualize the results of varying assumptions, explore consequences, and compare predictions with data. Mathematically proficient students at various grade levels are able to identify relevant external mathematical resources, such as **digital content located on a website**, and use them to pose or solve problems. They are able to use technological tools to explore and deepen their understanding of concepts.

We have provided lists of appropriate apps, websites, software, and lessons that will help you satisfy the standard for high school.

Your students will need to begin using technology as a tool to help them strengthen their math skills. That is essentially what this math standard—the only one that explicitly includes technology–states. Using technology as a mathematical practice tool can be interpreted in many different ways. In any case, technology is a math tool students should use as much as possible. Thankfully, there are many math programs, websites, and apps to choose from. The best of them have students learning in creative ways and are not just electronic worksheets. They automatically adapt to the students' skill levels, and they give you data that tells you where students are in their learning and what they need to effectively continue. Of course, these usually do not come free. Following are many good math resources. The free resources (many with ads) are often less interesting to students and not as well organized. They don't give you the feedback you need. However, you must make the decision about what is best for your circumstances and budget.

Following are some websites you can use to help students meet the ninth and tenth grade math standards.

WEBSITES FOR MATH

- **VirtualNerd (www.virtualnerd.com):** This is a free website with well-made videos on math subjects through Algebra 2 that you can use for instruction or to flip the classroom.

- **Khan Academy (www.khanacademy.org):** This nonprofit organization provides a free website with excellent activities at all age levels, including high school. Once logged in, you can keep track of student progress and data easily.

- **IXL (www.ixl.com/math):** This online site features adaptive individualized math through gameplay. This gives students immediate feedback and covers many skills, despite its emphasis on drills. Levels go to Algebra 2. Class price is $199/year.

- **EdHeads (www.edheads.org):** Real-world medical and engineering scenarios will intrigue kids on this free website. The site adeptly weaves content into authentic simulations. In-activity definitions and glossaries provide solid vocabulary support. There is no ability to monitor progress, and students can't fast forward/rewind within segments.

- **MathPickle (www.mathpickle.com):** This free website for Grades 5–12 is loaded with great math challenges, puzzling games, videos for flipping the classroom, and good ideas. There is a lot here, and you might need to guide your students through, unless they are very independent.

- **GeoGebra (www.geogebra.org):** Although it will take some time for teachers and students to learn how to use the site, if they are willing to put in the time,

GeoGebra offers endless math learning possibilities. The site is free and for Grades 7–12.

- **Desmos (www.desmos.com):** This website is a next-generation graphing calculator where students can use a "slider" to change to transform the function and see how that affects the graph. It is an elegant math tool that makes concepts more concrete, and it's free.

- **Get the Math (http://tinyurl.com/ne8fo6n):** This is a free website through PBS that uses video games, music, fashion, sports, restaurants, and special effects to teach math concepts. It is targeted for teenagers and has some great challenges, videos, and resources. It includes resources for teachers.

- **Radix Endeavor (www.radixendeavor.org):** This is multiplayer game play for STEM learning. Students are the players and play in the math or science strand. Teachers can enroll classes, but enrollment is not necessary for students to play this free online role-playing math game created at MIT.

- **TenMarks (www.tenmarks.com):** This website is adaptable to the student's math skill level. It is free for a single class, but schools and districts pay $20 per student for premium features. It has instruction, practice, and even assessment modeled after PARCC.

- **HippoCampus (www.hippocampus.org):** The ways to use this free website vary greatly. It has high school and college-level math, but also English, social studies, science, and even religion. There are also assessments, rubrics, teacher resources, tips about teaching, and so on. You must dig to find some of the great resources, but they are well worth it.

- **Gooru (www.gooru.org):** This is a free website with a supportive app that is also available free. The idea of the site is to share information and to make great resources available globally. They cover math, science, social studies, and language arts by providing videos, worksheets, assessments, and other resources for students broken out by each standard. Great for flipping the classroom. This is for Grades K–12.

- **Math Open Reference (www.mathopenref.com):** This is a free website with a myriad resources for teachers to use with their students to teach math. The site does have ads.

- **WebQuest (www.webquest.org):** WebQuests are great tools to use for presentations. WebQuest is a website, which allows students to follow an already-created, project-based lesson where information is found solely on the internet.

You can also create your own WebQuest if you have a website building program or a website like **Kafafa (www.kafafa.com/kafafa)**. **WebQuest.org** is the original and most popular site; however, if you search the internet, you will find more sites that you can use.

There are many affordable apps for high school math learners. Following is our short list.

APPS FOR MATH

- **Algebra Touch (www.regularberry.com):** This intuitive app makes learning algebra easy. Teachers can track students' progress, and it is especially good for struggling students. The price is $2.99.

- **iCrosss (http://tinyurl.com/phsouuf):** This $0.99 app will help students learn solid geometry in an easy and funny way. Spin and rotate shapes, and create cross sections to boost spatial understanding of geometric solids. There is no apparent developer website. Users must purchase this through app sites.

- **Clinometer (http://tinyurl.com/nkzww4g):** This $1.99 app for IOS and Android is used in measuring absolute angles and relative angles between device positions. It has speech synthesis and can display the slope in degrees, percentage, rise over run, and 1V:H (common in engineering). This is an ideal resource for a geometry class.

- **Algodoo (www.algodoo.com):** This free app is a virtual sandbox tool that helps your students play with the concepts of physics to design, construct, and explore.

- **Autodesk Digital STEAM Measurement (http://tinyurl.com/na3sn9h):** This app is free and shows students differing ways to measure quantity, dimension, time, temperature, capacity, weight, and mass in real-world situations. It is mostly interactive and teaches international units of measurement.

Literacy Lessons

Cross-curriculum planning is encouraged with the Common Core by using ELA standards in history, science, and technical studies. We highly encourage teaching more than one standard in the lesson, when you can. Getting through all of the standards you need in high school is very difficult in the time given. The key to planning with the CCSS is teaching multiple standards in one lesson and working together with others in your department and in other departments, if possible. With the following list of a few sample lessons for Grades 9–10, we hope that you will be inspired to become an effective technology lesson planner.

GATTACA

From the files of our high school friends, this assignment explores whether or not the movie Gattaca represents an accurate picture of what America will look like in the not-so-distant future. Students learn about biotechnology, DNA, and the genetics of inheritance as well as genetically engineered food (ground meat/hamburger in particular). The unit includes a lot of discussion through blogging—students are grouped across course sections for the discussion. First, students view the film Gattaca in class. Next, students are assigned to groups (across sections of the same course). In each class, students join the blog using Google Blogger. Articles and additional resources are found on the blog. Classmates are asked to discuss specific questions on the blog and to react to comments made by other group members. A Google Form is used as a way for students to document their participation.

Because the blog is active during the entire span of the unit, it allows students to post an opinion and then revise their thinking as a result of additional knowledge or opinions of others. This is the primary focus of **W.9-10.6** and **WHST.9-10.6**. As the class is organizing a complex topic, making corrections, and using formatting, multimedia, and graphics to help in comprehension, they are satisfying **W.9-10.2.A** and **WHST.9-10.2.A**. Students are making strategic use of digital media to enhance their understanding of the issues the movie presents, which satisfies **SL.9-10.5**, as well as integrating multiple sources of information in diverse formats (**SL.9-10.2**).

HISTORY OF TELEVISION

A local high school tenth grade English class spends time discussing and analyzing with students the television programming available to American families. After spending time discussing the history of television, students are divided into small groups and given an assignment to watch various television shows from each decade, using YouTube. Each team is assigned shows to watch so a different variety from each decade can be represented. You can generate your own list or have your students brainstorm a list with you. A list might include Jack Paar, Johnny Carson, Jackie Gleason, I Love Lucy, Bonanza, and so on. Teams next put together a Prezi or TouchCast to depict their show (genre, plot, characters, etc.). Some may even want to include a film snippet from their show, to give their audience an opportunity to see it. Next, presentations are shown to the class.

Discuss with your students their present-day experiences with television, as well as how much they know about producing a television show. Students divide into groups for this activity. Their first task is to spend some time researching and discussing how television programs are produced. Bring the class together to have a discussion on what each group discovered about television production. Each group will then develop an idea for their own show. First, they will write a proposal, describing the plot, setting, and characters, as well as the target audience. This can easily be written and shared with you using Google. Once the group is satisfied with their idea and you have given the go-ahead, they can begin writing their script for one episode of the show. It may be necessary for groups to research how television scripts are formatted.

After the script has been written, groups create a storyboard that shows the flow of the story in pictorial and written form. Use Google Storyboards for television scripts. There are a plethora of templates and examples students can use. Or, encourage them to create their own! Group members next choose actors for their show. After several rehearsals, they can begin putting their episode on video. Once all episodes have been completed, students share their creations with the entire class.

The primary focus for this lesson is **W.9-10.6** and **WHST.9-10.6**, by using the internet to produce, then update (revise) shared writing in a flexible way. They also satisfy **W.9-10.8** and **WHST.9-10.8** by researching using different sources, answering research questions, and integrating information. As the class is organizing a complex topic, making corrections, and using formatting, multimedia, and graphics to help in comprehension, they are satisfying **W.9-10.2.A** and **WHST.9-10.2.A**. They also integrate multiple sources of information presented in diverse media or formats (**SL.9-10.2**, as well as **SL.9-10.5**).

Science/Social Studies Lessons

The following sample lessons address CCSS ELA standards and teach lessons based on national standards in social studies and science.

WORLD RELIGIONS

The students in a ninth grade high school class compare the six major religions of the world. In this unit, you, as teacher, outline the major research questions. Students break into groups. Your class then completes research on the different religions using internet sites and school/public library databases. Next, students are asked what questions they still have, now that they have done the research. Their questions are sent to a representative for each religion (this particular high school found them through the school's career counselor). Each representative then is scheduled for a 30-minute presentation time to present to the class and answer the questions your class posed. Representatives either come to the classroom or are connected via a virtual meeting using Google Hangouts. Finally, your students compare and contrast the religions and revise their research for a better understanding.

The primary focus of this lesson is organizing a complex topic, making corrections, and using formatting, multimedia, and graphics to help in comprehension, so students are satisfying **W.9-10.2.A** and **WHST.9-10.2.A**. Also **W.9-10.6** and **WHST.9-10.6** is satisfied by using the internet to produce, then update (revise) shared writing in a flexible way. They also satisfy **W.9-10.8** and **WHST.9-10.8** by researching using different sources, answering research questions, and integrating information. They also integrated multiple sources of information presented in diverse media or formats **SL.9-10.2**.

WORLD SOCIAL ISSUES

Each year a nearby high school has their tenth graders grapple with world social issues to help students better understand political, religious, and economic issues. To complete this series of lessons, you might choose to have your students research countries that are participating in the Olympics. This knowledge then transfers to a larger unit during the fourth quarter, which requires your students to have a more extensive knowledge of a single country. The essential question for the fourth quarter learning would be, "Why do countries 'hate' the United States?" Your students are assigned a country to research, compare, and contrast. This is done under the umbrella of the Olympics. You would share overarching questions, which your students discuss, comment on, and then rethink.

The class can use apps such as Feedly to obtain current events about their country. Also, print media, videos, internet links, political cartoons, and so on are provided as source materials. When doing this, you would fulfill **RI.9-10.7** to analyze various accounts of a subject told in different mediums. Students must also compare and contrast text and other sources to note pros and cons and thus are satisfying **RST.9-10.9**. Students in your class can use Evernote, iAnnotate, or similar apps to help organize their sources and resources. That satisfies **WHST.9-10.6** by using technology, including the internet, to produce, publish, and update individual or shared writing products, taking advantage of technology's capacity to link to other information and to display information flexibly and dynamically, and **WHST.9-10.8** by gathering relevant information from multiple authoritative print and digital sources. Then your students can summarize their learning by using Google Docs or Slides, TouchCast, Aurasma, Mural, or other great sites and apps to create a presentation that is electronically posted for all to view, and review. This meets **SL.9-10.2** by integrating multiple sources of information presented in diverse media or formats and **SL.9-10.5** by making strategic use of digital media.

Math/Technical Subjects Lessons

Many teachers have embraced WebQuests as a way to make good use of the internet while engaging their students in a technology-rich environment for problem solving, information processing, collaboration, and the kinds of thinking that the 21st century requires. There are many WebQuests available for any high school subject, just by searching Google. WebQuests can be used all year. Once students are familiar with WebQuests, have them write their own!

BASEBALL ACTIVITIES

A neighboring high school starts the year with a WebQuest titled "Can You Buy a Winning Baseball Team?" You can find several versions of this WebQuest (already written) by searching the web with the title. Students work in teams and are presented with the problem: Major league baseball players are paid millions of dollars by team owners. Fans are questioning whether their favorite teams can compete with other teams. Is it possible for a team with a minimal payroll to win the World Series?

To answer these questions, students will need to collect the following data:

- The number of wins each professional baseball team had during the regular season in (pick a year).

- The total team payroll for each professional baseball team in (pick the same year as above).

- The population of each city with a professional baseball team (same as the year above).

Next, teams must put all data in a chart (Google Sheets, TouchCast, Glogster, etc.). Data should include the following:

- City population

- Attendance

- Team Payroll

- Number of regular-season wins

For this lesson, students will need a straightedge and graph paper, as well as access to the internet. Google online graph paper to check out the many options available. You can also use the Desmos website for graphing. You may want to give students sites that will be helpful to access the information they will need (see **our website** for this book, at **http://tinyurl.com/oexfhcv)**.

After teams have completed their research, they start to work on the following process.

1. Plot the numerical data on a coordinate plane three times:

   • Plot I: payroll versus wins

   • Plot II: population versus wins

   • Plot III: population versus payroll

2. Find a line of "best-fit" so most of the points are close to the ruler for each of the three graphs.

3. Plot the line, and then write an equation in slope-intercept form.

When all data has been plotted and graphed, students answer the following evaluation questions and submit to you via Google Docs or a similar program.

1. How much would you expect to pay a major league baseball team if you wanted them to win 100 games?

2. How many people would you expect to find in a city if the major league baseball team in that city won only 50 games?

3. Describe each of the three plots as having a positive correlation, negative correlation, or no correlation.

4. In Plot I, what does m value in the slope-intercept form represent?

5. In Plot II, what does the b value in the slope-intercept form represent?

6. What does the line on Plot I say about the relationship between the payroll of a major league baseball team and the number of games you can expect them to win?

7. What does the line on Plot II say about the relationship between the population of a major league baseball team's city and the number of games you can expect them to win?

8. What does the line on Plot III say about the relationship between the population of a major league baseball team's city and payroll of the major league baseball team in that city?

9. Examine your answer to #6 above. Some people are upset by this. Why?

10. Do you think all teams have an equal chance at getting to and winning the World Series? Why or why not?

Extra Credit: Do a team payroll versus wins versus population analysis of a different professional sport. You will need to answer all questions and complete all plots from above.

When all student teams have finished, come together as a class. Have a discussion and see if a consensus can be reached. Fans may be upset. They might know ahead of time that their team doesn't have a chance to win it all. At least that is the perception. Solutions to this problem are thrown around often (salary caps, removal of free agency), but because professional sports have become big business, the issue is becoming more complicated each year. What conclusion did your student team come up with? This would also be an excellent topic for a class blog discussion (Google Blogger, etc.).

In addition to **MP5**, using appropriate tools strategically, primary standards satisfied are **RI.9-10.7**, **RH.9-10.7**, and **RST.9-10.7**, as quantitative and technical analysis is needed to understand and determine the results for the teams. Also, **W.9-10.6** and **WHST.9-10.6** are satisfied when students share their data and debate the conclusion. These two standards are also addressed when students write, share, and publish their own WebQuests. Students are making strategic use of digital media to enhance their understanding of the data discovered in the WebQuest task, which satisfies **SL.9-10.5**, as well as integrating multiple sources of information in diverse formats (**SL.9-10.2**). Gathering relevant information from multiple digital sources, as well as assessing the usefulness of each resource to help plot the data and answer the research questions, satisfies **W.9-10.8** and **WHST 9-10.8**.

INCOME TAX ACTIVITIES

From the files of a local high school math coach, this lesson has students apply percentages to real-life situations by figuring the amount of income tax (federal, state, and local) that will be withheld from a salary for their "dream" job. Students will learn about credit and credit scores. They will learn what will hurt their scores and what will help their scores. Students will learn about all the aspects of credit, and that they will be able to make informed decisions regarding credit. Also, the concept of interest and how to analyze interest will also be addressed.

Students will use the internet to research salary information, as well as tax percentages for their area. This may be information you wish to provide for them, ensuring that all students have the same, accurate information. Math Standard **MP5** has students use appropriate tools strategically. You will need to decide if a calculator is appropriate for your students to use during this lesson. Most computers, laptops, tablets, and smartphones come equipped with a calculator. There are also free online calculators available.

Start the discussion with a survey of how many students have a credit card (or their parents), and if they understand how credit cards work. You may even want to consider doing a quick check of vocabulary, which will be addressed during the lesson. Terms like credit, credit card, credit risk, credit score, interest, APR, and credit limit are just a few suggestions to include in your lesson. You may wish to find videos to help you with this discussion (VirtualNerd, Khan Academy, MathPickle, etc.).

Next, have students research and report back to you (using Google Forms, Google Docs, or even a blog) by answering the following questions.

1. How do credit cards work?

2. How does credit card interest work, especially if you do not pay off the balance when the payment is due?

3. What is the difference between credit cards, debit cards, and cash, and how does each work?

4. What role do banks play in offering you credit?

5. What is a credit score? How do you get one? What makes up an individual's credit score? How do lenders use credit scores? How do private businesses use the scores?

6. Who calculates credit scores? The bank? Government? Private organizations? Give examples.

Once students have a solid foundational knowledge of salaries and taxes, they should think about their "dream" job. Explain they will have to pay taxes on that salary to the local, state, and federal government. They can research the tax percentages, or you can give the rates to them. Have them calculate how much each week, month, and year they will pay in taxes. Record the amount in a manner of their choice (Google Sheets, TouchCast, Glogster, Desmos, etc.). Once they have graphed the different amounts, have students draw conclusions about the taxes people pay. This can be written and submitted to you in a variety of ways (such as Google Docs, Google Blogger, or GoToMeeting).

Finally, your students can summarize their learning by using Google Docs, Prezi, TouchCast, Aurasma, Mural, or other great sites and apps to create a presentation that is electronically posted for all to view, and review. This meets **SL.9-10.2**, to integrate multiple sources of information presented in diverse media or formats, and **SL.9-10.5**, by making strategic use of digital media. Also, primary standards satisfied are **RI.9-10.7**, **RH.9-10.7**, and **RST.9-10.7**, as quantitative and technical analysis is needed to understand and determine the results for the teams.

Gathering relevant information from multiple digital sources, as well as assessing the usefulness of each resource to help plot the data and answer the research questions, satisfies **W.9-10.8** and **WHST.9-10.8**. **RI.9-10.6** is also satisfied when students analyze various accounts of a subject told in different mediums. Students in your class can use Evernote, iAnnotate, or similar apps to help organize their sources and resources. That satisfies **WHST.9-10.6** by using technology, including the internet, to produce, publish, and update individual or shared writing products, taking advantage of technology's capacity to link to other information and to display information flexibly and dynamically.

A Final Note

As students progress through the grades, they establish their baseline of proficiency in technology. This will definitely enhance students' experiences with technology in high school, as well as satisfy the CCSS performance standards at the 9–10 level. We hope that you found the resources and lesson ideas presented in this chapter useful and that they are easy to adapt to your class.

You will find more resources online at **our website (http://tinyurl.com/oexfhcv)**, which may be helpful to you as you look to differentiate your instruction. Visit our site for updated information about this book. To learn more about meeting technology standards found within the CCSS for other grades, look for our three additional titles in this collection.

Chapter 9

Practical Ideas for Grades 11–12

W e realize that you will want to focus on your particular grade or subject when you are planning your lessons and implementing CCSS, so we have organized the Practical Ideas chapters by grade level, then subject. Each grade starts with an overview followed by ELA technology standards with accompanying apps, software, and websites that you can use to help your students have success with that standard. We then continue with the math standard for the grade level and offer appropriate resources. Finally, we have included some sample lessons for each grade level in various subject areas. Although we intend for you to seek your specific grade and subject to help you implement CCSS for your students, please do not disregard other sections of this chapter. To see grades other than 9-12, look for our three additional titles in this series, as they could provide information to help you differentiate for your students.

The CCSS has been set up to encourage cross-curricular work in English language arts. It standardizes the writing process through all classes in freshman through senior year by bringing the same writing standard into history, science, and technical subjects. The CCSS in high school is divided in two: 9-10 and 11-12. As a high school teacher, you understand the difficulty of working with colleagues in other departments. There are systemic roadblocks that make communication with other departments difficult in most high schools, to say the least. But, co-designing lessons between the language arts teachers and the history, science, and technical teachers will be a significant step in helping to create a strong foundation for your students before they enter college. It is also important to work with your administrators to ensure that you have time to plan. Planning can take place during a school or districtwide professional development day or during staff meetings. Of course, the best option is to build collaboration time into the regular schedule.

Junior and senior students are the culmination of the Common Core State Standards mission that aligned the standards with college and career expectations. This is where the real test of success will take place. Are they ready for college? If they are not college bound, are they ready for a career? Of course, in the initial years, with the CCSS being implemented, success will most likely be harder to measure. In time, students coming to you will have had to measure up to Common Core standards each year, and should be coming to you more prepared each year.

The first few years of using the Common Core State Standards to teach will be like expecting your students to pilot a jet fighter, when they have all been trained to pilot prop planes. Sure, they are all still considered pilots, but the two experiences are very different things! And the new standards are just as different from those your school may have had previously. This class of students you now have before you was held to standards, but not Common Core State Standards. Therefore, there will be an adjustment that you must help them make, and knowledge and skills you need to backfill, for your students to be successful as the transition takes place. The CCSS has some major differences, which create an expectation that technology must be used when appropriate, and higher-order thinking skills need to be applied. These standards will be worth the extra time you will be spending now. The payoff will come as your students successfully enter college or a career having had these experiences.

Math is also an area where the technological tools become more varied and complex as students advance. The math standards are meant to be embedded in and a natural part of the units your students will be studying. Choosing the correct math tools will become an important part of your class's learning. There are wonderful new math resources available to help students become proficient in the standards.

Resources for Reading Literature

RL.11-12.7	READING LITERATURE

Analyze multiple interpretations of a story, drama, or poem (e.g., **recorded** or live production of a play or recorded novel or poetry), evaluating how **each version** interprets the source text. (Include at least one play by Shakespeare and one play by an American dramatist.)

THIS STANDARD BEGINS IN KINDERGARTEN with comparing illustrations and text and grows through the grades using all types of media to compare, support, and analyze their meaning. So, the standard is essentially to get meaning from more than text. Meaning can also come from all the accompanying media and even the format of the writing or media. The standard for Grades 11–12 differs somewhat from the same standard in Grades 9–10. As in this standard, freshmen and sophomores analyzed two things (art), but the end result was different. In Grades 9–10, they had to analyze what is emphasized and absent in each. At the 11th and 12th grade level, they need to analyze and then evaluate the different versions in relation to the source text.

The standard also includes the requirement that one of the plays studied be by Shakespeare, and another by an American dramatist. There are several sites that have excellent resources for Shakespeare and the complete collection of his plays. There are also some free resources for American plays. Of course, many movies, novels, songs, and poems are based on Shakespeare's plays, either directly or loosely. Moreover, many American plays have been made into movies. So, there are plenty of resources out there in which to immerse your students.

Your school district may subscribe to **Gale Literature Resource Center** or other Gale products **(http://tinyurl.com/o47ydvs)**. These are fine sources for thousands of frequently studied works. Your public library may have many digital resources that are free to your school district. Following are also some great media resources.

APPS AND WEBSITES FOR READING LITERATURE

- **Genius (www.genius.com):** This free website can be used to annotate everything from rap songs to Shakespeare. There is even an annotated Common Core to help teachers understand it better. You must sign up to post and add writing.

- **Folger Digital Texts (www.folger.edu):** This free, easy-to-search digital collection of online texts of the classics brings Shakespeare and other works into the digital age. Students can read them anywhere they have digital access.

- **Open Source Shakespeare (www.opensourceshakespeare.org):** This free, easy-to-search, digital online text brings Shakespeare's works into the digital age. Students can read them anywhere they have digital access.

- **The Complete Works of William Shakespeare (www.shakespeare.mit.edu):** This is another free, easy-to-search, digital online text with all of Shakespeare's works. Students can read them anywhere they have digital access.

- **Internet Archive (www.archive.org):** This site has more than 12 million books, films, audio files, photos, songs, and documents that are free to all. They come from libraries worldwide, TV stations, radio stations, and many other for-profit and nonprofit groups. Books include plays by Shakespeare and American classics.

- **Readbookonline (www.readbookonline.net/plays/):** This website with ads has 6,000 poems, essays, stories, and plays, many of the classics from Dickens, Shakespeare, Twain, and so on. It is a great free literature resource.

- **Edmodo (www.edmodo.com):** A free website where teachers can create a safe, password-protected learning community including blogs and sharing documents. A free app is available.

- **YouTube (www.youtube.com):** There are many free videos that your students can view, including literature, reviews of art, and endless other topics that might fit your curriculum. There is also a free app.

- **iTunes U (http://tinyurl.com/lbjbarh):** As stated on Apple's website, "Choose from more than 750,000 free lectures, videos, books, and other resources on thousands of subjects from Algebra to Zoology." It is accessed through iTunes free. There is a free iTunes U app available.

- **SchoolTube (www.schooltube.com):** This is the best free source for educators as a video sharing community where students can watch or post videos.

- **Netflix (www.netflix.com):** Filmed movies of classic literature, more current literature, and Shakespeare can be found at sites such as this. $8.99/month.

- **NeoK12 (www.neok12.com):** This is a website with short stories on video.

- **PBS Learning Media (www.pbslearningmedia.org):** This site is a great source for classroom-ready, free digital resources at all grades and in all subjects. This includes Masterpiece Theatre with accompanying lessons.

Resources for Reading Informational Text

RST.11-12.9	READING HISTORY, SCIENCE, AND TECHNICAL SUBJECTS

Synthesize information from a **range of sources** (e.g., texts, experiments, simulations) into a coherent understanding of a process, phenomenon, or concept, resolving conflicting information when possible.

IN THE READING STANDARD 9, the anchor standard is to analyze the similarity in theme in two or more texts. Although the 11-12 standard does not state the actual digital sources, the anchor standard does, and so it is implied that some of the sources must be videos and other media. In Grades 9-10, your students were to compare and contrast; the Grades 11-12 standard demands a bit more thought and a different process. But the differences do not end there. The Grades 9-10 RST standard 9 also required that students note support and contradictions in their comparison. In the Grades 11-12 version, as part of the synthesis, they must resolve any conflicting information. By this point in their studies, your class should have read history, social studies, science, and other disciplines extensively in previous grades. They would come to this standard with a good foundation of knowledge. The digital resources that follow are good jumping-off points in all areas of science, technical subjects, and history, including current events.

APPS AND WEBSITES WITH SOURCE MATERIAL

- **Learning Network (www.learning.blogs.nytimes.com):** This free website by the New York Times has many intriguing questions on current affairs that makes students think and analyze. The site contains multimedia and links to help students find more about issues and includes prompts for writing. There are ads.

- **CNN (www.cnn.com):** The Cable News Network site is free but includes ads. It has trending news events and access to text, pictures and video of current events.

- **The Washington Post (www.washingtonpost.com):** This is the official site of the leading newspaper in our capital. There is access to current events in the nation and world. The site is free, but it does have ads.

- **NPR (www.npr.org):** This site from National Public Radio is government sponsored and so is free with no ads. There are links to current stories with media. Students can watch the most current NPR Hourly Newscast.

- **MSNBC (www.msnbc.com):** A cable news site from NBC Universal, this free site does contain ads. You can find all the day's national and world news including video, photos, and text.

- **Newsmap (www.newsmap.jp):** Using visual mapping to focus on the hottest current issues makes this site like a "word cloud" for news. Each has links to the story behind the headlines. Articles provided by top news outlines around the world in this free online site.

- **Library of Congress (http://tinyurl.com/2knoku):** This site, as part of the Library of Congress's website, has easily searchable access to thousands of digital resources from the history of the United States. Free.

- **Feedly (www.feedly.com/i/welcome):** Organize any information on the web through this free app and website. It is a great resource for STEM to follow current events, scientific breakthroughs, and so on. Find and follow any source of information.

- **Flipboard (www.flipboard.com):** Similar to Feedly, but draws from some different resources. It is a free app that provides a wide range of information in a magazine format.

- **WatchKnowLearn (www.watchknowlearn.org):** The site has many free educational videos that allow you access to everything from frog dissection simulations to earthquake destruction. It organizes content by age ranges and provides reviews.

- **PBS Learning Media (www.pbslearningmedia.org):** This site is a great source for classroom-ready, free digital resources at all grades and in all subjects.

APPS AND WEBSITES TO SYNTHESIZE INFORMATION

- **Explain Everything (www.explaineverything.com):** This $2.99 app uses text, video, pictures, and voice to present whatever your students are asked to create. Students can animate, draw, or import almost any file and share multiple ways. It is a top app for a reason. Educational pricing is available.

- **Aurasma (www.aurasma.com):** You can use this free app to take a picture, website, and so on and add layers of animation to your original. They provide many resources, or you can use those that you create. It is great for getting information across in a quick, vivid, and animated way.

- **Corkulous (www.appigo.com):** This free app (Pro is $4.99) allows you to collaborate with friends and colleagues, manage project assignments, brainstorm, prepare or teach a lesson, take notes, and more. You can also export as a PDF.

- **Glogster (www.edu.glogster.com):** Presentations that you can create and share are available with this free app. You can browse and use those made by others. They provide images, graphics, videos, or upload your own. You must log onto the companion website. Teacher pricing of $39 $99/year is available.

- **Gooru (www.gooru.org):** This is a free website with a supportive app, also available also free. The idea of the site is to share information and to make great resources available globally. They cover math, science, social studies, and language arts by providing videos, worksheets, assessments, and other resources for students broken out by each standard.

- **Mural (www.mural.ly):** This website can help organize ideas quickly and display and share information with others. You can use visual aids for presentations, and it works with other apps and sites. The website does cost, but there is special yearly pricing for students ($49), teachers ($199), and schools ($999).

- **TouchCast (www.touchcast.com):** This cool software and app video creator lets you embed linkable websites, pictures, video, photos, and more into your video. It is free. There is some concern about privacy. TouchCast does have the EduCast channel, which is geared for education with teacher tutorials and other resources.

- **Zeega (zeega.com):** Easily combine media from the cloud to tell a story with video, audio, pictures, animation, and so on, to create a visual narrative. This mashup website is free, and students will enjoy the ease of this media-driven format to help get their story/poem/report message to others.

Resources to Integrate and Evaluate Information

RI.11-12.7	READING INFORMATIONAL TEXT

Integrate and evaluate multiple sources of information presented in **different media** or formats (e.g., visually, quantitatively) as well as in words in order to address a question or solve a problem.

RH.11-12.7	READING HISTORY

Integrate and evaluate multiple sources of information presented in **diverse formats** and media (e.g., visually, quantitatively, as well as in words) in order to address a question or solve a problem.

RST.11-12.7	READING SCIENCE AND TECHNICAL SUBJECTS

Integrate and evaluate multiple sources of information presented in **diverse formats and media** (e.g., quantitative data, video, **multimedia**) in order to address a question or solve a problem.

RI.11-12.7, RH.11-12.7, AND RI.11-12.7 are essentially the same standards and again focus on integration and evaluation when reading historical and technical texts. This standard begins in kindergarten with comparing illustrations and text and evolves through the grades to use all types of media to compare, support, and analyze the story's meaning. By freshman and sophomore year students analyze various accounts of a subject told in different mediums, but now, in Grades 11–12, the next step is to integrate and evaluate that information. Of course, they must put into practice their analytical skills from Grades 9–10 in order to master integration and evaluation of the information, which are higher-level thinking skills.

Integrating and evaluating needs to be taught through argumentation and teaching key questioning techniques. **Odell Education (www.odelleducation.com)** can help a great deal with techniques. Students and teachers can now link examples to specific text lines in published works. An overwhelming amount of what we hear and read today comes from people speaking and writing without proper support. There are many unsubstantiated opinions out there, and the CCSS attempts to force a speaker or writer to support what they say. Students can use text, embed images, links, and videos in their writing, integrating media not simply as an illustration, but as an integral part of the overall argument.

In the next section, we offer some useful apps, programs, and websites to help students become proficient at integrating and evaluating information.

WEBSITES FOR READING INFORMATION

There are many websites students can use to improve their reading skills. Following are a list of our favorites.

- **Feedly (www.feedly.com):** Organize any information on the web through this free app and website. It is a great resource for STEM to follow current events, scientific breakthroughs, and so on. Find and follow any source of information.

- **Google Scholar (http://scholar.google.com):** When your students conduct research, have them use Google Scholar by typing in "google scholar" on the Google search engine. This will bring up research, law papers, academic articles, and more on the topic they research.

- **Diigo (www.diigo.com):** With this free extension you add to your browser you can highlight, add a note or sticky, annotate, embed a website, and keep and organize everything you want. It is great for research and writing.

- **SpicyNodes (www.spicynodes.org):** This is an interesting three-dimensional mind-mapping website. It is paid or free, depending on what services you want. It is great for organizing and very effective for student memory retention. Nodes can contain links to URLs, links to other nodes, sound, pictures, and so on, for students to support their analysis.

- **Connected Learning (www.connectedlearning.tv):** This website is free, supported by the MacArthur Foundation. Connected Learning is working to change the educational process by making connections between students, their peers, the real world, student's interests, and education. What does this mean to you? This website is full of great resources and ideas. Each month they take on a new task to research.

- **Have Fun with History (www.havefunwithhistory.com):** This website is free and offers many short videos about historical events that can be used in the classroom. Some ads.

- **Digital Public Library of America (www.dp.la):** A free website that provides innovative ways to search and scan through the united collection of millions of items. You can search by timeline, map, virtual bookshelf, format, subject, and partner libraries.

- **Newsmap (www.newsmap.jp):** Uses visual mapping to focus on the hottest current issues. Each has links to the story behind the headlines. Articles provided by top news outlines around the world in this free online site.

- **Odell Education (www.odelleducation.com):** This site is a good source for ELA teacher resources. Everything there is free and sharable. Teachers can find well-researched step-by-step ways to implement Common Core standards in the area of student research.

- **PBS Learning Media (www.pbslearningmedia.org):** This website is a great source for classroom-ready, free digital resources.

- **WebQuests (www.webquest.org):** These are great tools to use for presentations. WebQuest is a website, which allows students to follow an already-created, project-based lesson where information is found solely on the internet. You can also create your own WebQuest if you have a website building program or a website like Kafafa **(www.kafafa.com/kafafa)**. **WebQuest.org** is the original and most popular site; however, if you search the internet, you will find more sites that you can use.

APPS FOR READING INFORMATION

- **Notability (www.gingerlabs.com):** This note-taking app allows your students to draw, using handwriting, typing, and importing text and other media. It allows markup of PDFs, too. It includes a word processor for essays, outlines, and forms. This app is $4.99.

- **Evernote (www.evernote.com):** A free app that helps you to create freeform notes, upload images, and make checklists. It is great for note taking. It can then sync your data across platforms.

- **Flipboard (www.flipboard.com):** Similar to Feedly, but with more constraints. It is a free app that provides a wide range of information in a magazine format.

- **Inspiration Maps (www.inspiration.com/inspmaps):** This $9.99 app helps students organize, plan, and build thinking skills as well as create and analyze charts and other data by producing a mind map that can include text, video, photos, audio, and so on. Volume discounts are available.

- **Explain Everything (www.explaineverything.com):** This $2.99 app uses text, video, pictures, and voice to present whatever your students are asked to create. Students can animate, draw, or import almost any file and share in multiple ways. You can link to other resources for supporting information. It is a top app for a reason. Educational pricing is available.

- **TouchCast (www.touchcast.com):** This cool software and app video creator lets you embed linkable websites, pictures, video, photos, and more into your video. It is free. There is some concern about privacy. TouchCast does have the EduCast channel, which is geared for education with teacher tutorials and other resources.

Writing Resources

W.11-12.2.A	WRITING *and*
WHST.11-12.2.A	WRITING HISTORY, SCIENCE, AND TECHNICAL SUBJECTS

Introduce a topic; organize complex ideas, concepts, and information so that each new element builds on that which precedes it to create a unified whole; include formatting (e.g., headings), **graphics** (e.g., figures, tables), and **multimedia** when useful to aiding comprehension.

W.11-12.6	WRITING *and*
WHST.11-12.6	WRITING HISTORY, SCIENCE, AND TECHNICAL SUBJECTS

Use technology, including the Internet, to produce, publish, and update individual or shared writing products in response to ongoing feedback, including new arguments or information.

W.11-12.8	WRITING *and*
WHST.11-12.8	WRITING HISTORY, SCIENCE, AND TECHNICAL SUBJECTS

Gather relevant information from multiple authoritative print and **digital sources, using advanced searches effectively;** assess the strengths and limitations of each source in terms of the task, purpose, and audience; integrate information into the text selectively to maintain the flow of ideas, avoiding plagiarism and overreliance on any one source and following a standard format for citation.

THE CCSS HAS STUDENTS EXPERIENCING informative or explanatory writing with standard 2 beginning in kindergarten. But, as they reach the high school level, they need to become college and career ready. In Grades 9–10, students had to make important connections and distinctions when satisfying standard 2. Students in 11th and 12th grade are to construct the written piece so that each element builds to a unified whole. As with Grades 9–10, an outlining program is a wonderful way for students to organize their ideas, concepts, and information so they can lay them out as building blocks of the unifying whole that is required. Several wonderful software programs have been used for mind-mapping and outlining for many years. However, there are also free sites out there.

Students from kindergarten to high school seniors need to become proficient in standard 6, which involves using technology to collaborate with others when writing. In ninth grade, for the first time, they were required to update their writing and to display information flexibly and dynamically. Updating their writing requires students to revise, react, and, in the case of argument, to rethink their position, when more information is found about the topic. Now as juniors and seniors, they need to learn how to update, in an ongoing way, by including new arguments and information gathered as they view, hear, and read more about the subject of their product. Updating is made easy with blogging and instantaneous feedback through technology. From this ongoing assessment of information, they may make a more informed decision, see it from other viewpoints, and sometimes draw different conclusions.

Writing Standard 8 starts in Grade 3 and continues through senior year in high school. This writing standard is keying in on the gathering of information, analyzing the information, and avoidance of plagiarism using multiple sources, digital as well as text, when writing informative or explanatory works. The standard changes significantly between sophomore and junior grades. Juniors and seniors will assess not just the usefulness of a source, but its strengths and limitations based on specific criteria (task, purpose, and audience.) Therefore, students will need to use techniques they have been honing, in both reading and writing, to identify the type of writing, audience, and its purpose and then assess it. Juniors and seniors also have a higher standard with regard to overreliance on any one source. They may have listed many sources in the past but only primarily used one or two. Now they need to pull information from all of their sources—if not equally, at least more equitably.

Following are some well-designed products that will help your students become more effective in the writing standards for these grades.

WEBSITES AND PROGRAMS FOR OUTLINING

- **iThoughts (www.toketaware.com):** Students can use this $9.99 mind-mapping app to organize their writing and presentation ideas. It has good import and export capabilities (PDF, PowerPoint, and other formats). This app can also be used as a whiteboard.

- **Inspiration Maps (www.inspiration.com/inspmaps):** This $9.99 app helps students organize, plan, and build thinking skills as well as create and analyze charts and other data by producing a mind map that can include text, video, photos, audio, and so on. Volume discounts are available. Their web-based version is called Webspiration (http://tinyurl.com/bmop3nh). $6/month.

- **Bubble.us (www.bubble.us):** This is a free (with limited use) mind-mapping website for Grades K–12. It can be shared by multiple students at a time and comes with an accompanying app. For more options, purchase a package for $6/month or $59/year. Both come with a 30-day free trial. Site licensing is available. Contact the company for specifics.

- **Mindmeister (www.mindmeister.com/education):** This is a free, basic mind-mapping website for Grades 2–12. Upgrades are available ($18/month for a single user; $30 per user for 6 months). Educational pricing is available for schools and universities ($6 per user for 6 months). All of the upgrades have a free trial period.

- **FreeMind (http://tinyurl.com/5qrd5):** This is a free mind-mapping tool for Grades 2–12. However, FreeMind is written in Java and will run on almost any system with a Java runtime environment. Options for a basic or maximum install are available.

WEBSITES FOR WRITING

In this next section, we offer some useful websites to help students become proficient in writing and note taking.

- **Google Drive (www.google.com/drive):** This website offers many useful tools for free, including the following.

  - **Google Docs:** This is a great product to use for your students. It makes collaboration easy, especially from home. Students are also able to add pictures and short video clips, tables, and charts. These can be used to enhance the development of the main ideas or theme of their writing or presentations.

- **Google Slides:** This is a simpler version of Microsoft's PowerPoint. Students can use this for sharing projects, summarizing their work, and peer-to-peer teaching.

- **Google Spreadsheet:** This tool can be used in many subject areas, to share data, charts, graphs, and other data for analysis of topics or issues.

- **Google Scholar (http://scholar.google.com):** When your students research, have them use Scholar found by typing in "google scholar" on the Google search engine. This will bring up research, law papers, academic articles, and more on the topic they research.

- **Google Sites:** Create your own website here. These are great for presenting ideas, interactive learning, and can be updated easily when data or events change.

- **Google Blogger (www.blogger.com):** This blogging site has more features than Edmodo. Students can see other classes and can be cross-grouped with similar sections of the same course by ability or with mixed ability as needed.

- **Google Form:** Great for checking student understanding instantly, for getting any kind of feedback on issues being studied, and for peer-to-peer teaching.

- **Google Drawing:** This provides your students a place to create art, illustrations, graphics, diagrams, and so on, to enhance presentations and meaning in their language, history, science, technical subjects, and mathematical work.

- **Add-ons:** Google has created many add-ons that can be attached to Doc, Spreadsheets, Blogger, Forms, etc., to add targeted functionality. One example is Doctopus. This add-on allows teachers to instantly distribute documents to their class, which then show up in each student's folder. They can then use those documents as a starting point in assignments, discussions, or practice.

- **Genius (www.genius.com):** This free website can be used to annotate everything from rap songs to Shakespeare. There is even an annotated Common Core to help teachers understand it better. You must sign up to post and add writing.

- **Connected Learning (www.connectedlearning.tv):** This website is free supported by the MacArthur Foundation. Connected Learning is working to change the educational process by making connections between students, their peers, the real world, student's interests, and education. This website is full of good resources and ideas. Each month they take on a new task to research.

- **Feedly (www.feedly.com):** Organize any information on the web through this free app and website. It is a great resource for STEM to follow current events, scientific breakthroughs, and so on. Find and follow any source of information.

- **Gooru (www.gooru.org):** This is a free website, with a supportive app also available for free. The idea of the site is to share information and to make great resources available globally. They cover math, science, social studies, and language arts by providing videos, worksheets, assessments, and other resources for students broken out by each standard. Great for flipping the classroom. This is for Grades K–12.

- **Folger Digital Texts (www.folger.edu):** This free, easy-to-search collection of online texts of the classics brings Shakespeare and other works into the digital age. Students can read them anywhere they have digital access.

- **Open Source Shakespeare (www.opensourceshakespeare.org):** This free, easy-to-search online text brings Shakespeare's works into the digital age. Students can read them anywhere they have digital access.

- **The Complete Works of William Shakespeare (www.shakespeare.mit.edu):** This is another free, easy-to-search online text with all of Shakespeare's works. Students can read them anywhere they have digital access.

- **Edmodo (www.edmodo.com):** A free website where teachers can create a safe, password-protected learning community, including blogs and sharing documents. This is a great way to get students to write daily. A free app is available.

- **Wikispaces (www.wikispaces.com):** A free website where teachers can create a safe, password-protected learning community including blogs and shared documents.

- **EasyBib (www.easybib.com):** Students can use this free website and app to generate citations in MLA, APA, and Chicago formats easily. Just copy and paste or scan the book's barcode.

- **TeacherBlogIt (TeacherBlogIt.com):** A free website where teachers can create a safe, password-protected learning community including blogs and sharing documents.

- **Learning Network (www.learning.blogs.nytimes.com):** This free website by the New York Times has many intriguing questions on current affairs that makes students think and analyze. The site contains multimedia and links to help students find out more about issues and includes prompts for writing.

- **Citation Machine (www.citationmachine.net):** This is a free website students can use to generate citations in MLA, APA, Turabian, and Chicago formats easily. Just copy, paste, and the website does the rest.

- **Purdue Online Writing Lab (http://tinyurl.com/n8r94uf):** This website was developed for college students but is available to all free. It has resources for any kind of writing, grammar, spelling, and mechanics.

- **CAST UDL Book Builder (http://bookbuilder.cast.org):** Use this nonprofit website to create, share, publish, and read digital books that engage and support diverse learners according to their individual needs, interests, and skills. The site is free.

- **Lulu (www.lulu.com) and Lulu Jr (www.lulujr.com):** These sites allow you to create real books and publish them online. Parents and students can purchase the books. The site is free to use, but a fee is required to publish..

- **Wix (www.wix.com):** This online website creator is drag-and-drop easy and includes templates. The basics are free. An app is available.

- **Webs (www.webs.com):** This online website creator allows you to choose a template and then drag and drop elements onto webpages. Basic functionality is free, and an app is available.

- **Kafafa (www.kafafa.com):** This is another online website creator that is drag-and-drop easy and includes templates. The website is $9.99/month for a class.

- **Weebly (www.weebly.com):** This online website creator is also drag-and-drop easy and includes templates. The basics, which include five pages, are free. There is even an app available.

- **Digital Public Library of America (www.dp.la):** A free website that provides innovative ways to search and scan through the united collection of millions of items, including by timeline, map, virtual bookshelf, format, subject, and partner libraries.

- **Newsmap (www.newsmap.jp):** Uses visual mapping to focus on the hottest current issues. Each has links to the story behind the headlines. Articles provided by top news outlines around the world online. Free.

- **Naviance (www.naviance.com):** Students can use this web-based service for college or career planning, personal learning plans, and getting their college documents organized and sent. Schools can use this service for family connections, help with admissions, and career guidance. The cost is over $2 per student, but there is a minimum and it can be expensive.

- **Odell Education (www.odelleducation.com):** This site is a great source for ELA teacher resources. Everything is free and sharable. Teachers can find well-researched step-by-step ways to implement Common Core standards in the area of student research.

APPS FOR WRITING

There are many apps that help to improve student writing skills. Following are a short list of options we recommend.

- **Turnitin (www.turnitin.com):** This free app allows teachers to grade student writing anywhere and also gives an "originality report" on the student's work automatically. Teachers can grade with an interactive rubric, embed comments and audio, and highlight sections of the writing.

- **Peer Edit (http://tinyurl.com/hxzp5xk):** Let your students edit each other's work and learn writing in the process. This $4.99 app provides an organized support system for students to be able to practice peer editing with writing samples.

- **Notability (www.gingerlabs.com):** This note-taking app allows your students to draw, using handwriting, typing, and importing text and other media. It allows markup of PDFs, too. It includes a word processor for essays, outlines, and forms. This app is $4.99.

- **iAnnotate (www.iannotate.com):** Similar to Notability, this app is primarily for note taking and markup of PDFs, PPT, and docs. It is a bit easier to import other formats in this app than in Notability. The price is $9.99.

- **Flipboard (flipboard.com):** Similar to Feedly, but with more constraints, and it draws from some different resources. A free app that provides a wide range of information in a magazine format.

- **iThoughts (www.toketaware.com):** Students can use this $9.99 mind-mapping app to organize their writing and presentation ideas. It has good import and export capabilities (PDF, PowerPoint, and other formats). This app can also be used as a whiteboard.

- **Pixton (www.pixton.com):** This intriguing online site is great for creating sophisticated comics where you can flexibly pose characters and change expressions and backgrounds, all while creating great dialog in story form. It is about $8.99/month per classroom, and there is also school or district pricing.

- **Explain Everything (www.explaineverything.com):** This $2.99 app uses text, video, pictures, and voice to present whatever your students are asked to create.

- **Evernote (www.evernote.com):** This is a free app that allows your students to share notes as well as audio and video recordings. It's very easy to use and share with other students as well as the teacher.

Speaking and Listening Resources

SL.11-12.2	SPEAKING AND LISTENING

Integrate multiple sources of information presented in **diverse formats and media** (e.g., visually, quantitatively, orally) in order to make informed decisions and solve problems, evaluating the credibility and accuracy of each source and noting any discrepancies among the data.

SL.11-12.5	SPEAKING AND LISTENING

Make strategic use of **digital media (e.g., textual, graphical, audio, visual, and interactive elements)** in presentations to enhance understanding of findings, reasoning, and evidence and to add interest.

SPEAKING AND LISTENING STANDARD 2 expects the use of technology from kindergarten through Grade 12. In today's world, we listen to all kinds of diverse media and constantly need to analyze and make decisions about its content. We also use multiple kinds of technology to speak to others. The idea behind writing standard 2 changes between sophomore and junior years. Specifically added is the need to integrate multiple sources of information to make informed decisions and solve problems. The Grades 9-10 standard in speaking and listening did not have students use sources to make decisions and solve problems. Students will now need to analyze their sources as to which is more valid, informed, opinionated, and so on, and, taking everything into consideration, also make decisions about the issue or problem, where they stand, why, and what might be done to solve the problem.

Also different is standard 2 in speaking and listening, from Grades 9-10 to junior and senior year. Students must evaluate the sources, noting any discrepancies among the data. Students will need to use **cloze reading skills (http://tinyurl.com/pk5ea7x)**, have a deep knowledge of their topic, and understand the data to find discrepancies. They will need to judge the pros and cons of each source and decide what weight to give the data, even with discrepancies, depending on the importance of the source.

Speaking and Listening Standard 5 is unchanged from Grades 9 and 10. Learning to use media to help in presentations is critical for college and career readiness. Your students need to make strategic use of digital media to enhance understanding for them and their audience. This highlights using technology effectively, not just using it because it is something "awesome."

APPS FOR PRESENTATIONS

Traditionally Microsoft PowerPoint has been the presentation program of choice, but it is costly. There is now a free single version called Microsoft Online that includes PowerPoint. Although this is still a great program to use, other, similar presentation programs have emerged. Apple offers **Keynote (www.apple.com/mac/keynote/)** as part of their computer software package, but the iPad/iPod version does cost. Its features are very similar to PowerPoint. Another program that has emerged is the free **Google Slides (www.google.com/slides/about/)**. There are other resources that help with presentations, such as Microsoft Draw (www.office.com) and **Google Drawings (www.google.com/drive)**. Microsoft Office is aimed toward business presentations; however, Google Drive products like Slides and Drawings are free and web based. Google Slides is also very easy to share, and multiple users can work on it at once, even from home, which makes this an especially good program to use when interacting and collaborating with others. You are also able to add audio recordings to your slides, as well as visual displays such as pictures and short video clips.

- **Teach by Knowmia (htttp://tinyurl.com/omd28eu):** This free app will help you create lessons with text, pictures, videos, drawing, and audio that can be shared with students, and students can create their own peer-to-peer lessons. All can be uploaded and shared via Knowmia's website.

- **Evernote (www.evernote.com):** This is a free app that also allows your students to share notes as well as audio and video recordings. It's very easy to use and share with other students as well as the teacher.

- **Prezi (Prezi.com):** You can sign-up for a free educational account, and your students can create and share presentations online. Prezi has mind-mapping, zoom, and motion and can import files. Presentations can be downloaded. A Prezi viewer app is available.

- **Glogster (www.edu.glogster.com):** Presentations that you can create and share are available with this free app. You can browse and use those made by others. They provide images, graphics, and videos, or you can upload your own. The companion website has teacher pricing of $39 to $99/year.

- **Explain Everything (www.explaineverything.com):** This $2.99 app uses text, video, pictures, and voice to present whatever your students are asked to create.

- **TouchCast (www.touchcast.com):** This cool and free app video creator lets you embed linkable websites, pictures, video, photos, and more into your video. It is also available on PC. There is some concern about privacy. TouchCast does have the EduCast channel, which is geared to education with teacher tutorials and other resources.

- **Aurasma (www.aurasma.com):** You can use this free app to take a picture, website, and so on and add layers of animation to your original. They provide many resources, or you can use ones you create. Great for getting information across in a quick, vivid, and animated way.

- **Corkulous (www.appigo.com):** This free app (Pro is $4.99) allows you to collaborate with friends and colleagues, manage project assignments, brainstorm, prepare or teach a lesson, take notes, and more. You can also export as a PDF.

- **BaiBoard (www.baiboard.com):** This whiteboard app allows students to create, collaborate, and share, and it's free. The difference with this and other whiteboard apps is that multiple students can have real-time access to one project and collaborate together.

WEBSITES FOR PRESENTATIONS

There are many web-based tools that students can use to create presentations. The following are a few of our favorites.

- **Google Blogger (www.blogger.com):** This free blog site has more numerous features. Students can see other classes and can be cross-grouped with similar sections of the same course by ability or with mixed ability as needed. An app is available.

- **Edmodo (www.edmodo.com):** A free website where teachers can create a safe, password-protected learning community including blogs and sharing documents. App available for free.

- **Wikispaces (www.wikispaces.com):** A free website where teachers can create a safe, password-protected learning community, including blogs and shared documents.

- **Google Slides (www.google.com/slides/about/):** This is a simpler version of Microsoft's PowerPoint, and it's free. Students can use this for sharing projects, summarizing their work, and peer-to-peer teaching.

- **Mural (www.mural.ly):** This website can help organize ideas more quickly and display and share information with others. You can use visual aids for presentations, and it works with other apps and sites. The website does cost, but there is special yearly pricing for students ($49), teachers ($199), and schools ($999).

- **Magisto (www.magisto.com):** It is surprising how easy it is to create a movie with this free app for all platforms. Creates movies with photos and videos. Add sound from your songs or theirs, and it does the rest.

- **Tiki-Toki (www.tiki-toki.com):** Make engaging timelines with this free website (there are ads). You can embed videos, share with others, add photos, use color coding, and add 3D effects. Upgrade (no ads and 50 student accounts) for $125/year.

- **Animoto (www.animoto.com):** This website allows you to turn your photos and music into stunning video slideshows. It offers HD, music, website links, and style screens. Educational use is free for unlimited videos of 20 minutes.

- **Capzles (www.capzles.com):** This free website has free apps to make it mobile. Students or teachers can create a digital presentation with video, photos, music, blogs, and documents.

- **Zeega (zeega.com):** Easily combine media from the cloud to tell a story with video, audio, pictures, animation, and so on, to create a visual narrative. This mashup website is free, and students will enjoy the ease of this media-driven format to help get their story/poem/report message to others.

- **Feedly (www.feedly.com):** Organize any information on the web through this free app and website. It is a great resource for STEM to follow current events, scientific breakthroughs, and so on. Find and follow any source of information.

- **Paper.li (www.paper.li)** and **Scoop.it (www.scoop.it):** Publish your own newspaper with these websites' access to sources, print as well as video. Then customize it for your audience. Share it to Facebook, Twitter, and so on. Free, but it costs for a Pro version with extra features.

- **SpicyNodes (www.spicynodes.org):** This is an interesting three-dimensional mind-mapping website. It is paid or free, depending on what services you want. It is great for organizing and very effective for student memory retention. Nodes can contain links to URLs, links to other nodes, sound, pictures, and so on.

MOVIE MAKING PROGRAMS, APPS, AND WEBSITES

Video editing programs and apps are numerous. Here are a few that we recommend for students in Grades 11–12.

- **iMovie and iMovie Trailer (www.apple.com/ios/imovie/):** This powerful program ($14.99) also comes as an app for $4.99. Students can use it to create presentations, movies, documentaries, and motion slideshows. Students can also create short (90-second) trailers that focus on important points about issues and events studied.

- **AndroVid (www.androvid.com):** Create a movie on an Android device. The free app is limited. The pro version is $1.99. Make a movie or slideshow, add effects, trim, cut, and add music. This app does most of what you want in a movie editor and is fairly intuitive.

- **Magisto (www.magisto.com):** It is surprising how easy it is to create a movie with this free app for all platforms. Creates movies with photos and videos. Add sound from your songs or theirs, and it does the rest.

- **Green Screen (www.doink.com/support/):** Create a green screen effect to put yourself or students in the story, video, photo, artwork, and so on with this app from Do Ink. Great for presentations. There is a timeline feature to edit presentations and mix audio and video layers. Saves to iPad. Cost is $2.99.

- **Windows Movie Maker (http://tinyurl.com/le5wemk):** This video editing program comes with Windows Essentials. You can import, edit, add music, and share your newly created video with others.

- **Adobe Voice (standout.adobe.com/voice):** Using your voice to tell the story, this free app from Adobe gives students and teachers a great way to make presentations. Create a movie without having to shoot one. The app provides photos, animations, and templates to organize the voiceovers.

- **Stupeflix (https://.studio.stupeflix.com/en)** Make free movies using your photos and videos for up to 20 minutes. It's very easy, and super fun!

- **TouchCast (www.touchcast.com):** This cool and free app video creator lets you embed linkable websites, pictures, video, photos, and more into your video. It is also available on PC. There is some concern about privacy. TouchCast does have the EduCast channel, which is geared for education with teacher tutorials and other resources.

Language Resources

> **L.11-12.4C** | LANGUAGE
>
> Consult general and specialized reference materials (e.g., dictionaries, glossaries, thesauruses), both print and **digital**, to find the pronunciation of a word or determine or clarify its precise meaning, its part of speech, its etymology, or its standard usage.

THIS STANDARD IS VERY straightforward, clarifying the meaning of words in all grade levels. Students need to know how to find word meanings using not just print but digital dictionaries, glossaries, and thesauruses. The standard changes slightly between Grades 9-10 and Grades 11-12, adding, "or its standard usage." The technology aspect of the standard is still the same.

DIGITAL DICTIONARY AND THESAURUS WEBSITES

Digital dictionaries and thesauruses are updated more often than their print versions, and they are very convenient to use. The more students use them, the more comfortable they will become. You should do lessons and activities to learn and practice how to find parts of speech, standard usage, and etymology with an online dictionary. Bookmark the following tools or put them on your website for easy access.

- **Merriam-Webster (www.merriam-webster.com):** A free digital dictionary for all ages. It is the most commonly used digital dictionary and includes a thesaurus.

- **WordSmyth (www.wordsmyth.net):** This site shows three levels of a student dictionary. When looking up a word, there are also links to a thesaurus and rhyming dictionary for that word. You can sign up for an ad-free version, which will not cost your school.

- **Word Central (www.wordcentral.com):** A student online dictionary that includes an audio pronunciation of the word as well as the definition. There are many teacher resources.

- **Thesaurus.com (www.thesaurus.com):** This is a great thesaurus site with many extra features. It does have some ads. Available online and as an app. Free.

- **Online Etymology Dictionary (www.etymonline.com):** This free site gives a detailed etymology for most words. There are several ways to search, from a single term to a whole phrase.

Math Resources

MP5	MATH

Use appropriate **tools** strategically.

THERE ARE TWO MAIN SETS of standards, processes and practices, for the Common Core Math standards. First, you have the math targets, written similarly to ELA (Number and Quantity, Algebra, Functions, Modeling, Geometry, and Statistics and Probability). While you work with high school students on math processes, such as algebra or modeling, you need to teach your students how to apply the Standards for Mathematical Practices (which include problem solving and precision) to those processes. One practice, the only one that includes technology, is mathematical practice 5, "Use appropriate tools strategically." Below is the explanation CCSS provides for **MP5**.

> Mathematically proficient students consider the available tools when solving a mathematical problem. These tools might include pencil and paper, concrete models, a ruler, a protractor, a **calculator, a spreadsheet, a computer algebra system, a statistical package, or dynamic geometry software**. Proficient students are sufficiently familiar with tools appropriate for their grade or course to make sound decisions about when each of these tools might be helpful, recognizing both the insight to be gained and their limitations. For example, mathematically proficient high school students analyze graphs of functions and solutions generated using a **graphing calculator**. They detect possible errors by strategically using estimation and other mathematical knowledge. When making mathematical models, they know that **technology** can enable them to visualize the results of varying assumptions, explore consequences, and compare predictions with data. Mathematically proficient students at various grade levels are able to identify relevant external mathematical resources, such as **digital content located on a website**, and use them to pose or solve problems. They are able to use technological tools to explore and deepen their understanding of concepts.

We have lists of below appropriate apps, websites, software, and lessons that will help you satisfy this standard for high school.

Your students will need to begin using technology as a tool to help them strengthen their math skills. That is essentially what this math standard—the only one that explicitly includes technology—states. Using technology as a mathematical practice tool can be interpreted in many different ways. In any case, technology is a math tool students should use as much as possible. Thankfully, there are many math programs, websites, and apps to choose from. The best of them have students learning in creative ways and are not just electronic worksheets. They automatically adapt to the students' skill levels, and they give you data that tells you where students are in their learning and what they need to effectively continue. Of course, these usually do not come free. Following are many good math resources. The free resources (many with ads) are often less interesting to students and not as well organized. They don't give you the feedback you need. However, you must make the decision about what is best for your circumstances and budget.

Following are some websites you can use to help students meet the eleventh and twelfth grade math standards.

WEBSITES FOR MATH

- **VirtualNerd (www.virtualnerd.com):** This is a free website with well-made videos on math subjects through Algebra 2 that you can use for instruction or to flip the classroom.

- **Khan Academy (www.khanacademy.org):** This nonprofit organization provides a free website with excellent activities at all age levels, including high school. Once logged in, you can keep track of student progress and data easily.

- **IXL (www.ixl.com/math):** This online site features adaptive individualized math through gameplay. This gives students immediate feedback and covers many skills, despite its emphasis on drills. Levels go to Algebra 2. Class price is $199/year.

- **EdHeads (www.edheads.org):** Real-world medical and engineering scenarios will intrigue kids on this free website. The site adeptly weaves content into authentic simulations. In-activity definitions and glossaries provide solid vocabulary support. There is no ability to monitor progress, and students can't fast forward/rewind within segments.

- **MathPickle (www.mathpickle.com):** This free website for Grades 5–12 is loaded with great math challenges, puzzling games, videos for flipping the classroom, and good ideas. There is a lot here, and you might need to guide your students through, unless they are very independent.

- **BizKid$ (www.bizkids.com):** Based on the Emmy Award–winning show, this free website helps teenagers learn about business and finances. The website has video clips, resources, lesson plans, and games that all teach applied math.

GeoGebra (www.geogebra.org): Although it will take some time for teachers and students to learn how to use the site, if they are willing to put in the time, GeoGebra offers endless math learning possibilities. The site is free and for Grades 7–12.

Desmos (www.desmos.com): This website is a next-generation graphing calculator where students can use a "slider" to change to transform the function and see how that affects the graph. It is an elegant math tool that makes concepts more concrete.

Get the Math (http://tinyurl.com/ne8fo6n): This is a free website through PBS that uses video games, music, fashion, sports, restaurants, and special effects to teach math concepts. It is targeted for teenagers and has some great challenges, videos, and resources. It includes resources for teachers.

Radix Endeavor (www.radixendeavor.org): This is multiplayer game play for STEM learning. Students are the players and play in the math or science strand. Teachers can enroll classes, but enrollment is not necessary for students to play this free role-playing math game created at MIT.

Shmoop (www.shmoop.com): You can work on math, language, SAT and ACT test prep, GED, STEM, and so on on this free website. It does have ads, but the site is appealing to teenage students and keeps track of their progress. Also, for a fee, you can upgrade and access more.

TenMarks (www.tenmarks.com): This website is adaptable to the student's math skill level. It is free for a single class, but schools and districts pay $20 per student for premium features. It has instruction, practice and even assessment modeled after PARCC.

HippoCampus (www.hippocampus.org): The ways to use this free website vary greatly. It has high school and college-level math, but also English, social studies, science, and even religion. There are also assessments, teacher resources like rubrics, tips about teaching, and so on. You must dig to find some of the great resources, but they are well worth it.

Gooru (www.gooru.org): This is a free website with a supportive app that is also available free. The idea of the site is to share information and to make great resources available globally. They cover math, science, social studies, and language arts by providing videos, worksheets, assessments, and other resources for students broken out by each standard. Great for flipping the classroom.

Math Open Reference (www.mathopenref.com): This is a free website with a myriad resources for teachers to use with their students to teach math. The site does have ads.

APPS FOR MATH

Math apps that are appropriate for high school students are numerous and relatively affordable. The following is a list of our recommended math apps.

- **Algebra Touch (www.regularberry.com):** This intuitive app makes learning algebra easy. Teachers can track students' progress, and it is especially good for struggling students. The price is $2.99.

- **Gizmos (www.explorelearning.com):** Use Gizmos, which are interactive digital tools, to teach specific math standards. This really helps students learn about complex concepts. This website by ExploreLearning has a free trial, but then you must pay. There is educator pricing. There is also a free app that can be used with a paid account.

- **iCrosss (http://tinyurl.com/phsouuf):** This $0.99 app will help students learn solid geometry in an easy and fun way. Spin and rotate shapes, and create cross sections to boost spatial understanding of geometric solids. And yes, there are three s's in iCrosss!

- **Algodoo (www.algodoo.com):** A free program and app that allows you to model geometry and physics. Students and teachers can create 2D simulations and can interact with their objects. They can add physics in the simulation, such as fluids, springs, hinges, motors, thrusters, light rays, tracers, optics, and lenses. Create graphs and visualize forces and momentum.

- **Geometry Pad (http://tinyurl.com/n3tfx4u):** Create fundamental geometric shapes, explore and change their properties with this free app. This will do just about everything a high school student needs to be successful in geometry. Geometry Pad+ is available for $6.99. There is no apparent corporate website.

- **isosceles+ (http://tinyurl.com/pzytsqz):** Use the tools to draw simple lines, circles, arcs, polygons, and so on to create complex drawings. This app is $4.99. The free version, isosceles, allows two drawings. The app is powerful enough to be used by teachers and professionals. There is no apparent corporate website.

- **Clinometer (http://tinyurl.com/nkzww4g):** This $1.99 app for IOS and Android is used in measuring absolute angles and relative angles between device positions. It has speech synthesis and can display the slope in degrees, percentage, rise over run, and 1V:H (common in engineering). Perfect for a geometry class.

- **Autodesk Digital STEAM Measurement (http://tinyurl.com/na3sn9h):** This app is free and shows students differing ways to measure quantity, dimension, time, temperature, capacity, weight, and mass in real-world situations. It is mostly interactive and teaches international units of measurement.

Literacy Lessons

Cross-curriculum planning is encouraged with the Common Core by using ELA standards in history, science, and technical subjects. We highly encourage teaching more than one standard during a lesson when you can. Getting through all of the standards you need in high school is very difficult. The key to planning with the CCSS is by teaching multiple standards in one lesson and working together with others in your department and in other departments, if possible. With the following sample lessons for Grades 11–12, we hope that you will be inspired to become an effective technology lesson planner.

CLASSROOM EXAMPLE

Our first example is more a model of a classroom style than a particular lesson. At our local high school, the English Composition class in 11th and 12th grade is a "paperless" composition class, which uses peer editing to a great degree. Assignments in this class are made using the Google Drive add-on Doctopus to distribute tasks, writing prompts, and other assignments. Students open the prompt or a blank sheet in Google Docs and share the assignment with their teacher. They then begin their work. If research is required, they use a variety of sources online or through the library. Students are able to access library databases through the internet. Students also access Google Scholar for some assignments.

The ability to peer edit each other's work using the share option in Google Docs is very important. Once completed, the assignment is checked for authenticity with Turnitin. The teacher is able to check progress throughout and use the comment feature to make suggestions. All work is graded online in Google Drive.

The primary focus of this lesson is organizing a complex topic, making corrections, adding appropriate sources, and using formatting, multimedia, and graphics to help in comprehension, so students are satisfying **W.11-12.2.A**, **W.11-12.6**, and **W.11-12.8**. Of course, the class satisfies all the technology Reading standards **RI.11-12.7/RH.11-12.7/RST.11-12.7**, Speaking and Listening **SL.11-12.2/SL.11-12.5**, and Language **L.11-12.4c** standards through their strategic use of digital resources to read, write, present, collaborate, and consult digital reference materials.

LITERATURE WEBQUEST

Many teachers have embraced WebQuests as a way to make good use of the internet while engaging their students in a technology-rich environment for problem solving, information processing, collaboration, and the kinds of thinking that the 21st century requires. There are many WebQuests available for any high school subject, just by searching Google. WebQuests can be used all year. Once students are familiar with WebQuests, have them write their own!

A local high school literature class starts the year with a WebQuest titled All Quiet on the Western Front. You can find several versions of this WebQuest (already written) by searching for the title on the web. Students work in teams of four. Teams will answer the essential question: What was it like to be a part of World War I? Next, teams are given the task of researching how different groups of people were affected by the Great War.

Students will then create an electronic presentation (of their choosing: PowerPoint, Keynote, Google Slides, etc.) and share it with you. This presentation will incorporate the information learned and draw conclusions about what it is like to experience war. Once groups have been chosen, teams must choose roles: a soldier, an officer, a civilian, or a woman involved in war work. Each member must choose a different role and follow the directions for that chosen person. Questions and answers for each role must be submitted electronically by individual team members. Once this step has been completed, teams may begin their presentation.

Following is a list of questions the students will need to consider.

1. Each team member needs to participate. How many slides should each team member create?

2. What person should the slides be written in? First? Third?

3. Should each slide contain information representing all four roles?

4. Do you want graphics or illustrations for each slide?

5. What information should the slides contain? For example, social status; living conditions; job during the war.

6. What else would you like students to explain about each role? A typical day in the life of their role?

7. Do you want a title slide? What should it contain?

8. Do you want students to include a resource slide that lists where images and information for the presentation was found?

Next, students work on tasks for their individual roles. Encourage students to use the links provided, search for additional material on their own, and find print material from the library to use, citing sources used. Speaking and Listening **SL.11-12.2/SL.11-12.5**, and Language **L.11-12.4c** standards are satisfied through students' strategic use of digital resources to read, write, present, collaborate, avoid plagiarism, and consult specialized reference materials.

Following are the four roles students have to choose from along with questions specific to each role.

Enlistee. You are about to enlist to fight in World War I as a soldier. You can use the links provided by us on **our website (http://tinyurl.com/oexfhcv)**, search on your own, and look for print sources to help you answer the following questions.

1. What country are you from? Why did you enlist?

2. What branch of the military are you in?

3. What is an average day like?

4. What are your assigned duties?

5. How did your assigned role change people who lived during World War I?

6. How did your role change the war?

7. What are some good things about your job? World War I?

8. What are some bad things about your job? World War I?

Pilot. You are about to be called up as an officer and will be sent overseas to fight in World War I. You can use the links provided on **our website (http://tinyurl.com/oexfhcv)**, search on your own, and look for print sources to help you answer the following questions.

1. What country are you from? What is your rank?

2. What branch of the military are you in?

3. What is an average day like?

4. What are your assigned duties?

5. How did your assigned role change people who lived during World War I?

6. How did your role change the war?

7. What are some good things about your job? World War I?

8. What are some bad things about your job? World War I?

9. Have you been in any battles? Which ones?

Private Citizen. You are a private citizen caught in the middle of the war. You can use the links provided on **our website (http://tinyurl.com/oexfhcv)**, search on your own, and look for print sources to help you answer the following questions.

1. Where do you live?

2. What do you (and your family) do for a living?

3. Have any battles been fought near your home?

4. What is an average day like for you and your family?

5. Did your country assign you and your family any duties? What are they?

6. What are some good things about World War I?

7. What are some bad things about World War I?

8. How has your life changed during the war?

9. How else are you helping the war efforts?

10. How do you feel about the war?

Nurse. World War I saw many medical personnel involved in the war effort. You volunteered to help the war effort as a nurse. You can use the links provided on **our website (http://tinyurl.com/oexfhcv)**, search on your own, and look for print sources to help you answer the following questions.

1. What organization do you work for?

2. Why did you choose to join the service?

3. Where are you stationed?

4. What country are you from? Why did you enlist?

5. What branch of the military are you in?

6. What is an average day like?

7. What are your assigned duties?

8. How did your assigned role change people who lived during World War I?

9. How did your role change the war?

10. What are some good things about your job? World War I?

11. What are some bad things about your job? World War I? Have you been aiding people in any battles? Which ones?

Students should refer to their research throughout the reading of the book. The goal of this WebQuest is to help students understand what it would have been like to be involved in the Great War. Students gain an understanding of what life was like for people involved in all sides of the conflict. While reading the book, continue the idea through class discussions and debates on the topic "What is the legacy of World War I?" Once students are familiar with WebQuests, have them write and publish their own for another novel!

In addition to **SL.11-12.2**, **SL.11-12.5**, and **L.11-12.4c**, all informational reading standards **RI.11-12.7/ RH.11-12.7/RST.11-12.**7 are satisfied by reading information using diverse media formats, as well as integrating and evaluating multiple sources of information in diverse formats. Organizing a complex topic, making corrections, adding appropriate sources, and using formatting, multimedia, and graphics to help in comprehension satisfy **W.11-12.2.A**, **W.11-12.6**, and **W.11-12.8**. These standards are also addressed when students write, share, and publish their own WebQuests. Gathering relevant information from multiple digital sources, as well as citing to avoid plagiarism and assessing the usefulness of each resource to help answer the research questions, satisfies **W.11-12.8** and **WHST 11-12.8**.

Science/Social Studies Lessons

The following sample lessons address CCSS ELA standards and teach lessons based on national standards in social studies and science.

RESEARCH ACTIVITY

In our local high school's AP Environmental Science class, students select a topic of interest, but this could be a model for any research in history, science or technical writing (e.g., Should water be sold in plastic bottles? Should public transportation in your hometown be increased?). Research is done by collecting data via a survey that uses Edmodo or some other survey site such as Google Form. The students also speak with local experts (if feasible) and conduct more global research using internet resources like Learning Network, Connected Learning, or Google Scholar and their library's databases.

The final product is presented using digital media, such as iMovie or Explain Everything. The presentation includes a statement of their belief after the research and a plan of action, and it includes live survey results, graphs, and research to support their point of view. Edmodo is also used to post links and videos that presenters wish to share.

The main standards driving this project are **WHST.11-12.2.A**, **WHST.11-12.6** and **WHST.11-12.8** to produce and publish a STEM writing project using digital technology. But, in 11th and 12th grade you must also "update individual or shared writing products in response to ongoing feedback, including new arguments or information." Using surveys and flexible apps and programs like Edmodo can assist ongoing feedback and make it easy to update on the fly. They are also fulfilling **RI.11-12.7**, **RH.11-12.7**, and **RST.11-12.7** by integrating and evaluating multiple sources of information to address a problem. **SL.11-12.2** and **SL.11-12.5** are satisfied by making the presentation of their findings using digital media.

CONSUMER EDUCATION

Our local students complete this is a lesson, called the Apartment Project, in Consumer Education class during the final years of high school. Several high schools in our area do this as a paperless project, using only tablets.

Student typically complete this activity as a group project where students select "roommates." Students choose their career after high school, additional training, or college. They then research their career, including future workplace projections, tasks, work environment, location, and estimated beginning salary, using free resources like the school's career counselor, free websites like the government's **Career One Stop (www.careeronestop.org)**, or paid services such as Naviance.

After this research is complete, and with teacher assistance, a realistic beginning salary is determined. Taxes are discussed and deducted from income. Ten percent savings are calculated. Then using Google Sheets and the internet (Zillow, Kelley Blue Book, auto websites) as well as primary interviews with adults, a budget is devised. Pie charts are created with Google Sheets to visually represent the percent of income for items. (Teachers explained parameters to students like comfortable percentages of income for housing, auto, food, utilities, etc.) Adjustments are made to live within the student's income. Presentations are made with Explain Everything.

This lesson checks off many of the technology standards. Primary standards satisfied are **RI.11-12.7**, **RH.11-12.7**, and **RST.11-12.7**, as quantitative and technical analysis is needed to understand and determine the economic realities for your students. Also, **WHST.11-12.2.A**, **WHST.11-12.6**, and **WHST.11-12.8** are satisfied by writing a shared product and analyzing different sources. Making informed decisions from the sources and presenting them to others in a natural outcome satisfies **SL.11-12.2** and **SL.11-12.5**. Finally, using Google Sheets, pie charts, analysis of budgets and taxes is an effective way to bring in the math standard MP5.

Math Lessons

MEASUREMENT

This next lesson comes from the files of the math coach at a local high school. Students use hands-on, real-life activities to practice measuring square footage, taking into account varying factors and making adjustments for them. This activity can be performed individually, in partners, or teams, and it gets students out of the classroom!

Students will need tape measures. Math Standard **MP5** has students use appropriate tools strategically. You will need to decide if it is appropriate for your students to use a calculator during this lesson. Most computers, laptops, tablets, and smartphones come equipped with a calculator. There are also free online calculators available. Next, share with students (Google Docs, Google Blogger, Google Hangouts, etc.) the problems they will be working to solve. Following are some examples.

1. Have students calculate the amount of concrete necessary to put a 4-foot walkway from one specific point outside on the school grounds to another.

2. Have students calculate the amount of carpet needed to cover a classroom, leaving a 3-foot band of tile all the way around.

3. Have students calculate the amount of fencing needed to surround an Olympic-size swimming pool, with a 3-foot deck all around.

Have students keep track of their calculations and notes, recording what they discover in a manner of their choice (Google Sheets, TouchCast, Glogster, Desmos, etc.). Once all students have finished their calculations, have them summarize their learning by using Google Docs, Prezi, TouchCast, Aurasma, Mural, or other good sites and apps that let students create a presentation that is electronically posted for all to view, and review. You may even wish to ask students for suggestions of things to measure!

In addition to **MP5**, the presentation portion of this lesson meets **SL. 11-12.2** (integrating multiple sources of information presented in diverse media or formats) and **SL.11-12.5** (making strategic use of digital media). Students may need to gather relevant information (such as equations specific to their given question) from multiple digital sources, to help them complete calculations related to their given questions (e.g., How big is a swimming pool? What is the common width of a sidewalk?).

They will also need to assess the usefulness of each resource to help record their data and answer the research question. When doing this, standards **W.11-12.8** and **WHST.11-12.8** are satisfied. They are also fulfilling **RI.11-12.7**, **RH.11-12.7**, and **RST.11-12.7** by integrating and evaluating multiple sources of information to address a problem. In addition, **RST.11-12.9** is satisfied, as students need to synthesize information from many sources to resolve conflicting information. Students in your class can use Evernote, iAnnotate, or similar apps to help organize their sources and resources. That satisfies **WHST.11-12.6** by using technology, including the internet, to produce, publish, and update individual or shared writing products, taking advantage of technology's capacity to link to other information and to display information flexibly and dynamically.

REAL WORLD PROBLEM SOLVING

This math lesson, again from the files of one of our high school friends, is used to teach real-world problem solving, involving any math concept. Students make a word problem video similar to those found at Virtual Nerd or Khan Academy, of real-world mathematical problems. If students prefer, they could also make a presentation involving a word problem. Working in pairs, students use a video or digital camera (a smartphone or tablet works as well) to take video or pictures of interesting objects around the school that has mathematical implications. Some suggested ideas include:

1. Tiles in the cafeteria or classroom

2. A stone or brick wall

3. Paper folding

4. Field of dandelions

5. Rate of acceleration

6. Testing gravity from a balcony

Using iMovie, Movie Maker (any other movie making software) or PowerPoint, Keynote, Google Slides, and so on, teams begin making their word problem videos or presentations. Teams may wish to research some ideas and examples from VirtualNerd or Khan Academy before beginning. Next, students write their real-life word problem to go along with their pictures or video.

At the appropriate time, have students project their movie and "teach" the class. "Learning" students solve the problems and/or take necessary notes using Evernote, Diigo, Explain Everything (which they can use written and voice recorded notations), and so on. Teams present (BaiBoard, RealtimeBoard, etc.) to the class, making sure they save time for asking and answering any questions, as they are "the experts" on the problem. These movies and presentations can then be uploaded to YouTube or your favorite posting site to share with absent students and/or parents. They can then be revisited any time during the year. Encourage students to continue looking for examples throughout their daily life, writing a problem, and posting them for others to solve. This is a good idea for flipping the classroom as well.

In addition to math standard **MP5**, they are also fulfilling **RI.11-12.7**, **RH.11-12.7**, or **RST.11-12.7** by integrating and evaluating multiple sources of information to address a problem. Students are introducing, producing, and publishing writing, as well as working together to present their ideas clearly and efficiently, so **W.11-12.2A/WHST.11-12.2A**, **W.11-12.6/WHST.11-12.6**, and **W.11-12.8/WHST.11-12.8** are also met. **RI.11-12.7** and **W.11-12.7** are also satisfied when students gather, integrate, and present their information, in an original way. Using diverse media and formats (including music, graphics, voiceovers, etc.) to present and clarify information is definitely a part of this project, so **SL.11-12.2** and SL.11-12.5 are also fulfilled.

A Final Note

As students progress through the grades, they are establishing their proficiency in technology, finally culminating in their readiness for college or a successful career. There are many good ideas in this chapter that you may be able to adapt to your class. Satisfying the CCSS performance standards at the 9–12 level will give our students a greater chance of success as adults in the "real" world. You will find more resources online at **our website (http://tinyurl.com/oexfhcv)**, which may be helpful to you for differentiation as well. We hope you will visit our online site for updated information about this book. To see grades other than 9–12, look for our three additional titles in this series.

References

DeWitt, P. (2013, July 7). *Take a risk . . . Flip your parent communication! [Blog post]. Retrieved from http://blogs.edweek.org/edweek/finding_common_ground/2013/07/take_a_risk_flip_your_parent_communication.html*

Edutopia. (2007). What is successful technology integration? *Technology Integration Professional Development Guide.* Retrieved from http://www.edutopia.org/technology-integration-guide-description

Henderson. A., & Mapp, K. (2002). *A new wave of evidence: The impact of school, family, and community connections on student achievement* (Annual Synthesis 2002). Retrieved from Southwest Educational Development Laboratory website: http://www.sedl.org/connections/resources/evidence.pdf

LEAD Commission. (2012). *Parents' and teachers' attitudes and opinions on technology in education.* (National online survey, August 2012). Retrieved from LEAD Commission website: http://www.leadcommission.org/sites/default/files/LEAD Poll Deck.pdf

Meeuwse, K. (2013, April 11). *Using iPads to transform teaching and learning* [Blog post]. Retrieved from http://iteachwithipads.net/2013/04/11/using-ipads-to-transform-teaching-and-learning

National Governors Association Center for Best Practices, Council of Chief State School Officers. (2010). *Common Core State Standards. Washington, DC: Authors.*

New York University. (2007) *National Symposium on the Millennial Student.* Retrieved from http://www.nyu.edu/frn/publications/millennial.student/Millennial.index.html

Partnership for 21st Century Skills. (2004). *The partnership for 21st century skills—Framework for 21st century learning.* Retrieved from http://www.p21.org/about-us/p21-framework

Sammons, L. (2009). Guided math: a framework for mathematics instruction. Huntington Beach: Shell Education.

Sammons, L. (2011, September 21). Guided math: a framework for math instruction. Retrieved June 25, 2015, from http://www.slideshare.net/ggierhart/guided-math-powerpointbytheauthorofguidedmath

Strategic Learning Programs. (n.d.). Retrieved from http://www.iste.org/lead/professional-services/strategic-learning-programs

Swanson, K. (2013, October 1). Tips for explaining common core to parents—*THE Journal. Retrieved from http://thejournal.com/2013/10/01/how-to-explain-common-core-to-parents.aspx*

Szybinski, D. (2007). From the Executive Director - NETWORK: A Journal of Faculty Development. Retrieved from http://tinyurl.com/pqwr7va

United States Congress. (2010) Section 1015c. Chapter 28: Higher education resources and student assistance. In *Title 20–Education* (2010 ed.). Retrieved from http://www.gpo.gov/fdsys/pkg/USCODE-2010-title20/html/USCODE-2010-title20-chap28.htm